The
Paths of Life

and
Other Addresses

Volume 19

CHARLES A. COATES
1862 - 1945

Scripture references are generally from the King James Bibles unless otherwise noted.

* * * * *

Page numbering does not correspond to the published index of C.A.C.'s ministry. This is because larger type and page sizes affect the pagination.

This edition is published by:

BIBLES, etc.
www.bibles-etc.com

Layout by: W.S.Chellberg
February 2021

ISBN: 978-0912868-29-5

Available from:
www.LuLu.com

Biography of Charles Andrew Coates

This book is part of a large series from original sources of published ministry given over many years by Charles A Coates, who was born in Bradford, England, in December 1862, and died in Teignmouth, Devon in October 1945.

He relates that he started writing and publishing tracts at the age of 22, and by 1900, books collecting his lectures and writings began a limited private circulation. Interest led to more general publication of several collections included in this series. His ministry is now widely appreciated and has been frequently republished. Mr Coates may be best known for a series of Outlines of many books of the Bible. These are later than the collected tracts and lectures, being based on notes of Bible readings from 1920 up until shortly before his death, almost all of which were revised by him. A lot more of his ministry has been published since his death.

Mr Coates' ministry reflects his long life of devoted service to the Lord, and the depth and extent of his love and appreciation of divine truth. It is valued for its clarity and accessibility, and many have been drawn into the study of the Word by starting with one or other of his books. He cuts in a straight line the word of truth; not only accurate in his interpretation, but also direct and faithful in the application of the truth to our walk and conduct. He is sound on the foundations of the gospel, giving extensive guidance and assurance to souls seeking establishment in their faith.

Walter Brown sums up Mr Coates in this introduction to his published letters -

> Our brother's active service was for many years much restricted through bodily weakness, and this contributed, under the Lord's hand, to the development of ... choice spiritual feelings. His mind was remarkably formed by the teaching of the Holy Scriptures, and all that he wrote was the result of prayerful consideration. Hence the combination of unswerving faithfulness to the Lord with true humility and gracious sympathy in the spiritual experiences of others. Above all else, the reader cannot fail to remark in these pages our beloved brother's deep appreciation of the Person of Christ, and his wholehearted devotedness to His interests on earth, centring in "His body, which is the assembly". No matter affecting the Lord or His saints was regarded as too trivial for his interest and

prayers, and the smallest service done for His Name and glory found recognition and appreciation.

Charles Coates was born and brought up in Yorkshire. His father, James Coates, was born in Scotland in 1809. James is said to have once been a shepherd, but from no later than 1841, he was a linen draper in Bradford. He was moved to withdraw from the Congregational Chapel there in 1846 to be among the brethren in the town; and in 1855 was married to Elizabeth Rollinson, born in nearby Otley in 1820.

Charles was converted at the age of 16 – a turning point he marked by writing the first of several hymns. Sometime before his mother died in 1905, he moved with her to Paignton, Devon. After she died, he had lodgings in Teignmouth, and lived and broke bread there until his death. He never married. Mr Coates started working with his father as a draper, but evidently gave this up -perhaps when his father died: his health was poor from an early age. His infirmity also limited how much he travelled, so that much of his ministry was either given locally, or written.

This set of books is published with the desire that others may find and get the benefit of what the Lord gave His people through our brother; and that this will be to God's glory.

D. Andrew Burr
February 2021

CONTENTS

"THE PATHS OF LIFE"

Proverbs 1; Proverbs 2

I trust it may be helpful to us all, and especially to the young believers present, to look at the divine principles which are set forth in these chapters. I need hardly say that we do not get the light of Christianity in the book of Proverbs; but we get principles and encouragements and warnings which can be viewed now in the light of Christianity, and which are full of instruction. We see in principle the characteristics of those who take hold of "the path of life", and how they are delivered from "the ways of darkness".

In the first place, "The fear of the Lord is the beginning of knowledge" (1:7). The natural man cannot know the things of God, because he lacks that which is "the beginning of knowledge" - there is no fear of God before his eyes (Romans 3:11, 18). This being the case, it is evident that there must be a work of God in man to prepare him for the reception of divine knowledge. The new birth is an absolute necessity. A man who is "born anew" has the fear of God before his eyes, and he begins to look at things from an entirely new standpoint. The natural man judges of things without any reference to the will of God; he does what he likes - so far as he has opportunity - and is a god to himself, He may be moral or religious, if that be the bent of his mind; but he does not really fear God, and therefore has neither a just sense of what sin is, nor a true appreciation of grace.

The one "born of water and of the Spirit" hates evil (see Proverbs 8:13), though he may have to say, "What I hate, that do I" (Romans 7:15), and he hates it because it is displeasing to God. "By the fear of the Lord men depart from evil" (Proverbs 18:6). It is this holy fear that causes those born anew to cease practising evil and to separate themselves from the company and ways of the ungodly, thus bringing forth "fruits meet for repentance". It also causes them to abhor themselves because they discover that sin dwells in them, and that in them - that is, in their flesh - dwells no good thing (Romans 7:18).

But, on the other hand, "In the fear of the Lord is strong confidence: and his children shall have a place of refuge. The fear of the Lord is a fountain of life, to depart from the snares of death" (Proverbs 14:26, 27). Those who fear God are always marked by confidence in Him, of which prayer is the expression. That it can be said, "Behold he prayeth", is one of the first and surest signs that a divine work has begun in a soul. It is man - the needy and guilty sinner - turning to God for relief and refuge and salvation. The fear of God never leads a man to despair, but to "strong confidence" in God, so that however vile and guilty he may have been, he has an instinctive sense that he may look to God with confidence for pardon and salvation from the power of evil. The fear of the Lord thus becomes "a fountain of life", for it not only causes a man to hate evil and to depart from the snares of death, but it turns him to God as the Source of life and every blessing.

Then, "His children shall have a place of refuge" is very full of meaning if we connect with it (as we surely may) the thought of all that is provided for man by the grace of God through our Lord Jesus Christ. He has made atonement by the sacrifice of Himself, and God has raised Him from the dead; and now the forgiveness of sins is preached in His Name, and by Him all who believe are justified from all things. Such was the gospel preached by Paul at Antioch to those who feared God (Acts 13). Judaism stood condemned by its rejection of Christ, and the heathen world was fully ripe for the judgment of God. But there was then, and there is now, "a place of refuge" for those who fear God. CHRIST is made known, in the day of His rejection by Israel, as the Saviour of the world. It is not a Christ accepted and honoured here - a Christ after the flesh - whom we have to do with. It is a Christ rejected and crucified here, but who has at the moment of His entire rejection by man accomplished redemption, and who is now raised again and set at God's right hand. He has been in the place of evil, as made sin for us, so that everything contrary to God might come under judgment. Evil has neither been ignored nor compromised in any way. It has been fully dealt with according to divine holiness in the death of Christ, so that grace might reign through righteousness. And Christ risen is the glorious Witness that redemption is accomplished, that sin is judged, that sins are purged, that God is glorified, that grace is triumphant, and, in short, that God as a Saviour God has removed every barrier that stood in the way of man's blessing.

All this is now proclaimed in the gospel, and "made known to all nations for the obedience of faith". Those who believe find "a place of refuge" in God Himself - revealed in grace as a Saviour God. The gospel tolerates no mixture of self-righteousness or self-confidence in any form; God alone is the confidence and boast of His children. And as He alone is the refuge of His saints, so His thoughts and His love are the only measure of their blessing. It is of the greatest importance that we should be simple in our sense of *grace*, and that we should not allow the enemy to divert us from it. To turn back to the consideration of ourselves - our feelings, works, attainments, etc. - or to suppose that religious observances, sacraments, and law-keeping are necessary or advantageous in addition to Christ and the grace of God received by faith, is really to leave the ground of Christian blessing and to become fallen from grace (see the Epistle to the Galatians). The gospel by which we were begotten to the knowledge of God was a gospel of absolute grace, and it brought to our hearts the joy of blessings conferred by pure grace. It was no question of what we were, or of what we could do, but of what *God* was, and what *God* would do for the gratification of His own heart.

In connection with this we may apply the principle of the words, "My son, hear the instruction of thy father, and forsake not the law of thy mother: for they shall be an ornament of grace unto thy head, and chains about thy neck" (Proverbs 1:8, 9). We have been begotten by the testimony of grace. Whatever servant or instrument God might be pleased to use, it was the testimony of His grace by which we were begotten, according to 1 Peter 1:23-25, "Being born again, not of corruptible seed, but of incorruptible, by the word of God, which liveth and abideth for ever. For all flesh is as grass, and all the glory of man as the flower of grass. The grass withereth, and the flower thereof falleth away, but the word of the Lord endureth for ever. And this is the word which by the gospel is preached unto you". In this sense the testimony of Grace is our father, while "Jerusalem which is above" - the whole blessed system of heavenly grace which is established and set forth in Christ in glory - "is the mother of us all" (Galatians 4:26). The Galatians were slipping quite away from the gospel by which they had been begotten, and had "fallen from grace". They had, for the time, become deaf to the instruction of their father, and had forsaken the law of their mother, and the result was that they had lost their ornaments of grace. They must have quite lost the sense of sonship, and lacked the "fruit of the Spirit". If we depart from grace we depart altogether from God, and from everything which can maintain freshness, power, and spiritual joy in our souls. In short, we lose our divine ornaments, and drop down to the level of religious flesh.

It is as being "under grace" that we can walk in liberty and joy in the fear of the Lord. The fear of the Lord is the practical recognition in the soul that we are now to be here for God's will and not our own. Just as self-will is characteristic of the flesh, the fear of the Lord is characteristic of those born of God. It is really the spirit of obedience and subjection to God. It has been said that "obedience is the only exercise, save praise, of life to God". As we walk in the fear of the Lord, under His eye and in subjection to His will, we get practical deliverance from mere human expediency and from the motives and principles of action which control men in the world.

I put it to every one here, Do you know the grace and love of God, so that you can trust Him with your happiness? You have trusted Him for the eternal blessing of your soul, but can you trust Him with your happiness day by day? A desire may arise in your mind for something that you would not like to pray for. Now you may be quite sure that anything you cannot pray for, and that you cannot receive from God in grace and love, will not minister in the smallest degree to your true happiness. God would have our confidence in Him to be so strong that we should be afraid to touch anything that we could not take as directly from Him. It was so with our blessed Lord. The devil said, "If thou be the Son of God, command this stone that it be made bread". Was not bread a good thing for a hungry man? Had He not power to do what was suggested? Yes, indeed, but He would not depart from subjection to God. He would not make a loaf for Himself without a word from God. He set Jehovah always before Him.

While walking in the fear of the Lord, and with godly exercise, it is deeply important that we should keep very simple in the sense of grace. We fail in many things, and then the enemy seeks to take away the sense of grace, so that distance may come in between us and God, But

GRACE IS SUPREME,

and as we know this we are encouraged to go straight to God even when we have failed. He is "the God of all grace". We have to "judge ourselves", but we do so in the presence of infinite grace. The lowest point in the universe is death, and we see grace there, for Jesus "by the grace of God tasted death". The highest point is the throne of God, and grace is seen in glory there, for Jesus is there. So Christ fills all things in the moral universe, and we cannot look at any point between the dust of death and the throne of God's glory without seeing there the blessed witness of grace. How this encourages confidence in God as "the God of all grace"!

There is an important word here which I commend to every young believer. "My son, if sinners entice thee, consent thou not" (Proverbs 1:10). The secret of many an unhappy and unfruitful life can be found in the inability to say "No". If you want an accomplishment that will be of practical service to you as a Christian, cultivate the power to say "No". There are many sinners around, and there is also a sinner within, ready at all times to entice you from "the paths of life". They only consult to cast you down from your excellency, and to move you away from your true happiness. You must not parley with them; you must not compromise; you must say "No". When a neighbour, or acquaintance, or fellow-worker in the shop or the office asks you to go here and there for worldly pleasure, or offers to lend you a worldly book, that is the time to say "No". It does no good to get out of such things by making excuses. If you make excuses they will keep on at you, but if you quietly and graciously tell them you cannot do as they desire, and why, it is very probable that they will not trouble you again.

Then, as I have said, there is a sinner within. The desires and tastes of the flesh may often appeal for gratification. The flesh in us is as fond of the things of the world as ever. The first qualification of a disciple of Christ is the ability to say "No" to himself. "If any man will come after me, let him deny himself, and take up his cross, and follow me" (Matthew 16:24).

Then we get the voice of wisdom addressing itself to men (Proverbs 1:20-33). Every divine testimony is the voice of wisdom, and if men be willing to hear that voice, and to turn from their sin and folly, the Spirit of wisdom is poured out unto them, and wisdom's words are made known to them. The voice of wisdom today is the gospel of God concerning His Son Jesus Christ our Lord, and those who hear it receive the Holy Ghost. It is when we have heard wisdom's voice, and received wisdom's Spirit, that we are free in conscience and heart to make wisdom, understanding and knowledge the great object of our pursuit and search. "My son, if thou wilt receive my words, and hide my commandments with thee, so that thou incline thine ear unto wisdom, and apply thine heart to understanding; yea, if thou criest after knowledge, and liftest up thy voice for understanding; if thou seekest her as silver, and searchest for her as for hid treasures; then shalt thou understand the fear of the Lord, and find the knowledge of God" (Proverbs 2:1-5).

I greatly desire that all our hearts may be attracted by the blessedness of this. The world's philosophers profess to be searching for wisdom, but with them it is a mere abstraction - certain conceptions of their own minds in which they can take pleasure. For those born of God wisdom is set forth in the Person of Christ, the Son of God, and God would have us to enrich our souls by searching out the priceless treasures that are enfolded in Him. He is "unto the Jews a stumbling-block, and unto the Greeks foolishness; but unto them which are called, both Jews and Greeks, Christ the power of God, and the wisdom of God" (1 Corinthians 1:23,24).

We read that wisdom was with God "from the beginning, or ever the earth was ... Then I was by him, as one brought up with him: and I was daily his delight, rejoicing always before him; rejoicing in the habitable part of his earth; and my delights were with the sons of men" (Proverbs 8:23; Proverbs 8:30,31). Would you not like to know more of the Person in whom God's wisdom is now presented to men? More of the blessed One whose heart was so set upon you that He would go to the cross to die for you, that He might have you for and with Himself for ever?

Christ is the wisdom of God in view of all the questions which sin had raised, and which appeared to make the blessing of man and the accomplishment of the purposes of divine love impossible. How perfectly has God solved every problem and removed every difficulty, taking away in holy judgment by the death of Christ the man in whom sin had fully displayed itself, so that Christ in resurrection might be the Head and Centre of a new world for God's pleasure and glory! Christ is the wisdom of God for all this; and not only do we see in Him a resource which was more than equal to every difficulty that stood in the way of love's eternal purpose, but we also find in Him the perfect and blessed revelation of God. "No man hath seen God at any time; the only begotten Son, which is in the bosom of the Father, he hath declared him" (John 1:18). To "find the knowledge of God" is the great prize set before us, to be sought as silver and searched for as for hid treasure (Proverbs 2:4, 5). And where can this be found, save in the beloved Son who "declared him" here, and in whose face as the risen and glorified One all God's glory shines?

Now I should like you to note three things which characterize the one whose heart is set upon the acquisition of "wisdom". First, he has wisdom's Spirit. Of this we have a distinct intimation in Proverbs 1:23. I do not think anyone goes after Christ with much spring and energy of soul, or becomes very deeply affected by a desire to have "the knowledge of God", until he has received the Spirit. To believe the gospel and to receive the Spirit by the hearing of faith is the beginning of our Christian history; but it is only the beginning. We have to come under divine teaching, and to feed upon proper spiritual food, in order to grow and be formed in divine capacity to understand divine things. And this is subsequent to the reception of the Spirit. Nothing can be more injurious to souls than the supposition that they have reached full Christian stature because they have the Spirit. I admit that every one who has the Spirit is complete, just as a new-born babe is complete. But the babe must feed and grow in order to come to full stature, and so must the saint.

True growth is by the knowledge of God revealed in His beloved Son. It is of Him that the Holy Ghost ever delights to speak. "He shall teach you all things, and bring all things to your remembrance, whatsoever I have said unto you" (John 14:26); "He shall testify of me" (John 15:26); "He shall glorify me: for he shall receive of mine, and shall show it unto you. All things that the Father hath are mine: therefore said I, that he shall take of mine, and shall show it unto you" (John 16:14, 15). We have received wisdom's Spirit that we may be interested in these blessed things, and capable of apprehending them. "The anointing which ye have received of him abideth in you, and ye need not that any man teach you: but as the same anointing teacheth you of all things, and is truth, and is no lie, and even as it hath taught you, ye shall abide in him" (1 John 2:27).

The Father has been perfectly revealed in the Son, and now the Holy Ghost abides in us as a divine anointing, to teach us to find the fulness of grace and truth in Him. Everything that constitutes "wisdom" is to be found in Christ. People sometimes talk about "development" in Christianity, but everything that goes beyond, or is added to Christ is really apostasy; it is simply departure from the truth and is of the father of lies. The effect of having wisdom's Spirit is that we find all truth - everything that constitutes "wisdom" - set forth in Christ the Son of God.

But, having such an unction to teach us, how is it that we have not gained more of the knowledge of Christ? We know much of other things, but oh! how little do we really know of Christ! How is this? I think we may find the answer by looking at the second characteristic of those who are set upon getting "wisdom".

"My son, if thou wilt receive my words, and hide my commandments with thee; so that thou incline thine ear unto wisdom, and apply thine heart to understanding" (Proverbs 2:1, 2). It is necessary that we should have *the inclined ear and the applied heart*. The ministry of Christ is maintained here in the power of the Spirit, but often we fail to get the good of it because we lack interest in it.

Did you ever go to see a believer when your heart was full of something you had got from the Lord, the joy of which you were longing to share with some fellow-saint, only to find that his mind was preoccupied with other things, so that there was no response to what you were saying - no real interest in the matter? Did you not feel hindered and grieved, and did you not come away with a heavy heart? Methinks that is how the Holy Ghost feels oftentimes with us. He looks for us to have the inclined ear and the applied heart. We may be sure that Rebekah was as anxious to hear about Isaac as Eliezer was to tell her about him. Oh! that it might be so with us!

We need not suppose that wisdom's voice is silent today. In wonderful grace God has maintained and revived the ministry of Christ amongst His saints. To this end gifts have been given - "some, apostles; and some, prophets; and some, evangelists; and some, pastors and teachers; for the perfecting of the saints, for the work of the ministry, for the edifying of the body of Christ" (Ephesians 4:11, 12). It is wonderful how the Lord has maintained in ministry amongst His saints that which is really the voice of wisdom, especially when we consider how numerous and powerful are the influences which tend to silence that voice.

None of us here can say that God has failed to bring before us in ministry that which is of Himself - the ministry of Christ. The question is, Have we had the inclined ear and the applied heart? If believers - young or old - do not get enlarged in the knowledge of Christ, it is not because help and ministry are lacking, but because they have not the inclined ear and the applied heart. Some would like to be helped without the trouble of paying any attention to divine things. From sheer spiritual idleness or indifference they starve in the midst of plenty.

No one set upon the acquisition of "wisdom" would fail to "give attendance to reading". "All scripture is given by inspiration of God, and is profitable for doctrine, for reproof, for correction, for instruction in righteousness: that the man of God may be perfect, thoroughly furnished unto all good works" (1 Timothy 4:13; 2 Timothy 3:16, 17). We may be sure that a man who neglects Scripture has neither the inclined ear nor the applied heart. But let us make sure that meditation and prayer and holy exercise go along with our "reading". "Meditate upon these things; give thyself wholly to them; that thy profiting may appear to all" (1 Timothy 4:15). Do not read too much, or you will find that it becomes a mere mental exercise. I came across an old farmer one day in trouble about a cow which he said was "off her cud", in consequence of having eaten too much the day before. If you read beyond your power to meditate it will do you no good. It is better to get a little that we can meditate upon than a great deal merely in the way of information.

The third characteristic of those who are set to get "wisdom" is prayer. "If thou criest after knowledge, and liftest up thy voice for understanding; if thou seekest her as silver, and searchest for her as for hid treasures; then shalt thou understand the fear of the Lord, and find the knowledge of God. For the Lord giveth wisdom: out of his mouth cometh knowledge and understanding" (verses 3-6). God does not give us what we do not want, but He fills the hungry with good things, and satisfies the longing soul. If we seek spiritual blessing from God, we shall surely get it. Ministry is not of very much value to those who are not seeking and searching for God's "hid treasures", though, of course, God may use ministry to awaken exercise and desire. Do we pray in secret for more knowledge of Christ? We may read the Word and pray for comfort in our circumstances of sorrow or difficulty; we may read and pray in connection with our service; but, beloved brethren, how much do we in secret long after the deepened knowledge of God?

The great gain of having wisdom is set forth in verse 5, "Then shalt thou understand the fear of the Lord, and find the knowledge of God". "The fear of the Lord" practically excludes the world, and the flesh with its lusts. It shuts out all that is of ourselves according to the flesh. Then "the knowledge of God" brings in everything that is excellent and blessed for the endless satisfaction of our hearts. This, in a word, is "wisdom". We recognize that all that is of ourselves is evil, and we "judge ourselves", but while doing so we find infinite blessedness in the knowledge of God revealed in His beloved Son. We "rejoice in Christ Jesus, and have no confidence in the flesh".

Then, as to the path down here, it is a comfort to know that the Lord "preserveth the way of his saints" (verse 8). We shall meet with hindrances, difficulties, and obstacles. Satan will do his best to stop us - to tell us that there is a lion in the way - but the way of God's saints will be kept open by divine power to the end. The path may become narrower as Christendom drifts into open apostasy, but it will be wide enough for the faithful one to have the Lord at his right hand all the way through, so that he shall not be moved. To the faithful ones in Philadelphia He reveals Himself as having the key of David to open and shut, and He says, "I have set before thee an open door, and no man can shut it" (Revelation 3:8). He will to the end preserve "the way of his saints".

The effect of having "wisdom" is that we "understand righteousness, and judgment, and equity; yea, every good path" (verse 9). It is by "the knowledge of God" that we understand "every good path", for as we become more acquainted with Him we learn what is suited to Him. It is not that we have a code of rules to regulate our conduct, but we grow by the knowledge of God in the understanding of what is pleasing to Him, and thus we are preserved from all that is evil here, and we take hold of "the paths of life".

The two great forms of evil are represented by "the evil man" and "the strange woman" (Proverbs 2:12,16). "The evil man" represents the active energy of evil, or positive self-will; "the strange woman" sets forth the seductive power of evil. As we get "wisdom" we become really afraid of our own will. It is a terrible thing when self-will works in a believer, because it puts him in conflict with God, and must result in soul-misery and the loss of all joy. Well might the psalmist pray, "Keep back thy servant also from presumptuous sins; let them not have dominion over me" (Psalm 19:13). Self-will is like a demon which, when it is allowed to have dominion, carries a man on in utter disregard of the will and pleasure of God.

Then "the strange woman" is more the seductive power of evil. It is the secret, subtle, and often unsuspected influence by which souls are turned away from the guide of their youth and from the covenant of their God. The world often attires itself in a religious garb in order to beguile saints, and many fall into the snare. Little things, and seemingly innocent things, come in one by one. There is no sudden breakdown to alarm the conscience. The course does not seem to be much changed, but gradually and surely the believer is altogether diverted from "the paths of life".

But by having wisdom we get deliverance both from "the evil man" and "the strange woman". God is before us - well known in all-blessing grace and love - and as grace reigns in our hearts the power of self-will is broken.

> *"The Father's love with joy we own,*
> *Revealed in Christ the Son". (Hymn 178)*

And this displaces the world in our affections. We escape the snares by having Christ before us. We do not need to discuss the right or wrong of everything that presents itself; it is enough for us that it is "not after Christ". Thus our "eyes look right on" and we "turn not to the right hand nor to the left". We take hold of "the paths of life", and in those paths we walk safely and with God, and find true blessing for our souls.

———

MARKS OF WISDOM'S CHILDREN

Proverbs 3:5-12; Proverbs 4:23-27

Deep is the joy, and great the peace, of wisdom's children who walk in her ways, "for her ways are ways of pleasantness, and all her paths are peace". Gloominess of spirit and a melancholy visage are not among the marks of wisdom's children; they are rather indications of self-occupation, and clearly show that the soul has not yet crossed what a dear aged servant of the Lord used to call "the vanity line". All that is of the world and of ourselves as in the flesh is "vanity", and if we look to find satisfaction in that quarter we shall be grievously disappointed. The death of Christ has drawn the line, and proved that there is nothing in the world or in man after the flesh for God. On the other side of the "vanity line" is a new world called "the things of the Spirit", and the centre of that world is Christ risen and glorified at the right hand of God. There is no "vanity and vexation of spirit" in that world, and wisdom's children have their life there.

But if in heart and spirit we have "crossed the line", we are still, as to bodily presence and actual condition, in a world where wisdom has not her home - where she is a stranger walking in ways and paths of her own. And her children are known by the fact that they walk in her ways, turning not aside at the seductive invitation of the world, nor straying into bypaths and crooked ways. The instincts of wisdom's children lead them to walk in her ways, but they have also wisdom's guidebook in which all her ways are accurately marked, and every bypath carefully pointed out, so that they are without excuse if they go astray. Tonight, with wisdom's guidebook in my hand, I should like to call your attention to five marks of wisdom's children.

1. DEPENDENCE

"Trust in the Lord with all thine heart; and lean not unto thine own understanding". Dependence is no way of pleasantness and peace to an unconverted man; it is a dreadful moment to him when he is compelled to realize his dependence on God; he never turns to God unless he is in dire extremity - on a sinking ship or something of that kind. The reason of this is that he has no confidence in God. There is nothing more galling than to be dependent on someone we have no confidence in; and on the other hand, nothing gives such rest and peace to the heart as dependence, if there be perfect confidence in the person on whom we depend.

Dependence is the first lesson in the school of God; it is the way of our earliest blessing. We had to be entirely dependent on God for pardon, assurance, peace, and all the blessings which filled our hearts with the joy of salvation; so long as we leaned to our own understanding we got nothing.

As I have said, there can be no happy dependence if there is not confidence. Now what is the first mark of confidence in God? To find the answer to this question let us read Psalm 32:6: "I acknowledged my sin unto thee, and mine iniquity have I not hid. I said, I will confess my transgressions unto the Lord; and thou forgavest the iniquity of my sin". God had put His hand upon David, and brought conviction of sin into his conscience, but for some time he "kept silence"; he had not confidence in God. It is the power of darkness and unbelief that keeps a man silent when he is feeling the burden of his sins. The devil says, Don't think that a man like you will get anything from God; and the unbelieving heart only too readily accepts the foul lie that is intended to keep it in distrust of God. But the first mark of wisdom's children is that they justify God; that is, they are prepared to own their sin and guilt without reserve before Him, because they have confidence in His grace. They recognize His holy hatred of sin, but at the same time they give Him the honour and glory of His grace (see Luke 7:29-35).

I think it must be a great surprise to the devil when a man, crushed under the burden of his sins, turns to God about them. I do not think the devil can understand a sinner having confidence in God. He knows nothing of grace himself, and cannot understand its actings either for sinners or in them. Distrust of God makes the sinner hide from Him, as Adam and Eve did in the garden, but when Grace has wrought confidence in God in the soul the sinner turns to God. As Augustine said, the difference between a sinner and a saint is that the sinner hides from God and the saint hides in God. The first true sign of confidence in God is that we go to Him about our sin, and uncover it in His presence. When a sinner uncovers his sin before God, he learns how, in infinite grace, God can cover it. The word "hid" in verse 5 is the same as "covered" in verse 1. To such a man "God imputeth righteousness without works", and this "through the redemption that is in Christ Jesus" (Romans 4:6; Romans 3:24). God has secured for Himself in righteousness the title to abound in grace towards every guilty sinner who turns to Him.

I trust we all understand something of having this confidence in God; but let me remind you that it is of deep importance that it should be maintained all the way through. When failure comes in, and in many things we all offend, it is always Satan's effort to undermine our confidence in God - to keep us from turning at once to God about it. "I have prayed for thee, that thy faith fail not", said the Lord to His disciple who was so soon to deny Him (Luke 22). The great thing for us when we fail is to turn at once to God about it. That is the true secret and power of holiness. The man who has such confidence in the grace of God that he turns to God at once about his sins is a holy man. The man who says he has not sinned for a week is a self-deceived hypocrite. Having to do with God is the true power of holiness, and this is based on confidence in Him.

Then as to our circumstances and the difficulties of the path. If we are not walking in dependence we are walking in self-will and sin. If we had more confidence in God we should be more in the spirit of dependence about everything. Perhaps you may say, I should like to have more confidence in God, but how am I to get it? You must get to know Him better. The way to get our faith increased is by increasing our knowledge of God. Make it the supreme business of your life to get better acquainted with God. He has told Himself out; He has expressed Himself fully. All that God is has come out in the Person of His Son, and by the cross, so that we may know Him in the depths of His grace and love. He has loved us and does love us with all His heart, and the answer to that love, when it is truly known, is that we trust Him with all our heart. Unreserved love, when it is known, produces unreserved trust. "They that know thy name will put their trust in thee". As to His care, He feeds the fowls, clothes the lilies, thinks of every individual sparrow, and has numbered the hairs of our heads. As to His *love*, He spared not His own Son, but delivered Him up for us all. As to His purpose, He will have us to be conformed to the image of His Son in glory. As to His wisdom, He has pledged Himself to make all things work together for good to them who love Him, and who are called according to His purpose. Why should we not trust Him? Has He not done everything to win and retain the confidence of our hearts?

"And lean not unto thine own understanding". I remember a man who came round professing to cure people of rheumatism, and the first thing he did was to break the crutches of those who went to him. He wanted people to trust him altogether for a perfect cure, and this may serve to illustrate the point of the verse before us. wisdom's children do not lean on the natural crutches to which unbelief clings. The man of faith uses his brains, it is true, for natural things, but he does not trust them. He knows that he may consider and calculate, and take everything into account which could have weight with his "own understanding", and, having used his best judgment, be quite wrong in his conclusions and decisions. He lives on another principle altogether; he walks "by faith, not by sight".

In olden times mariners never went out of sight of land, and it was an immense advance when they ventured to embark on the high seas, trusting the chart and compass alone. The

Word of God is the chart for wisdom's children, and their compass is a simple faith which ever turns with steady purpose to the Lord.

2. DIRECTION

"In all thy ways acknowledge him, and he shall direct thy paths". I am afraid that guidance is looked upon by many as a very uncertain and unreliable kind of thing. There is no uncertainty about it. If the conditions are fulfilled on our side, there is always direct guidance for us. The conditions are just what I have already spoken about - dependence and confidence. Our chief concern should be that we are in a state to be guided.

A believer's course indicates where he is in his soul, and sooner or later exposes the motives that control him. It is pretty easy to see when a man has the Lord before him. You find him regulated by divine motives, and ordering his ways with reference to the will of God and the interests of Christ. He will not be occupied with guidance, but his whole course will evidence that his steps are ordered by the Lord. On the other hand, if a man be carnal and worldly, it will come out in his ways. He will have no divine judgment about things - no spiritual sensibilities or tastes - and, though he may maintain a certain degree of outward correctness, it will be manifest that he is not guided by the Lord. It is in having to do with the Lord that we are enlightened and our spiritual intelligence developed, so that we are enabled to discern the path that is pleasing to Him. God would guide us, as a rule, by forming our souls in the intelligence of His will, and thus enabling us to exercise a spiritual judgment about things.

Many would like to have guidance without any reference to their spiritual condition; but this is never the Lord's way. I have often been amazed at the devices to which even converted people will resort in a moment of perplexity. A favourite plan is to open the Bible at haphazard, or put a pin between the leaves, and read the text which happens to turn up. This savours more of witchcraft and superstition than of godliness. As we go on with the Lord, and become acquainted with His mind, our vision is cleared in a wonderful way. When Moses pitched the tent of meeting outside the camp, he had no direct word of guidance, but his judgment had been formed in the presence of God, so that he knew what was the fitting thing to be done. This is the great thing to be exercised about. To be guided by the knowledge of God and by an intelligent acquaintance with the mind of the Lord is a much greater thing, morally, than being directed how to act by an oracular utterance.

It has been truly said that a great deal of exercise about guidance is caused by our self-importance - *we* are so much objects of consideration to ourselves, and our doings, our movements, etc., are so much before us. None of us are very important personages after all, and probably the Lord intends most of us to tread a quiet and simple path without looking for any extraordinary and special guidance; and yet in blessed assurance that He cares and considers for us, and orders, prevents, and over-rules in a wonderful way for those whose hearts confide in Him. Mark the connection in which guidance is spoken of in Psalm 32: "For this shall every one that is godly pray unto thee in a time when thou mayest be found" (verse 6). Here we get dependence; the grace that forgives iniquity and covers sin, puts the soul on praying terms with God. Then, further, "Thou art my hiding place; thou shalt preserve me from trouble; thou shalt compass me about with songs of deliverance" (verse 7). Here we see unquestioning and unwavering *confidence*. Now, what follows? The Lord comes in and answers the confidence thus expressed by saying, "I will instruct thee and teach thee in the way which thou shalt go: I will guide thee with mine eye" (verse 8). The two "Thou shalts" of Confidence are answered by the two "I wills" of divine guidance. The Lord will not fail us; we may count upon Him; but to have this guidance we must be near to Him in confidence and in true subjection of spirit to Himself. If confidence and subjection are lacking, we become "as the horse or as the mule, which have no understanding: whose mouth must be held in with bit and bridle" (verse 9). The Lord does not, even in that case, give us up; He keeps His hand upon the reins, and uses circumstances to check, restrain, and direct us. But this is sorry and painful work compared with the blessedness of being guided by His eye.

Jude puts the conditions and the result beautifully together, "But ye, beloved, building up yourselves on your most holy faith, praying in the Holy Ghost". The Holy Ghost would ever maintain us in a dependent spirit, which is the secret of true stability. Then, "Keep yourselves in the love of God, looking for the mercy of our Lord Jesus Christ unto eternal life". Here we are viewed as in the confidence of divine love both in the present and as to the future. And what follows? "Now unto him that is able to keep you from stumbling, and to present you faultless before the presence of his glory with exceeding joy, to the only wise God our Saviour, be glory and majesty, dominion and power, both now and ever. Amen". I understand this to mean that if we were preserved in absolute dependence and confidence, the power of God would be so exercised on our behalf, and we should be so guided, as never to have a stumble all the way to glory. *He* is "able" and willing to do this for us - great as it is - if there is on our part dependence and confidence in Himself. "In all thy ways acknowledge him, and *he shall direct thy paths*".

3. DEVOTEDNESS

"Honour the Lord with thy substance, and with the firstfruits of all thine increase: so shall thy barns be filled with plenty, and thy presses shall burst out with new wine". Devotedness is the expression of the fact that the Lord has His right place in our affections. I suppose every Christian would accept this as being true; but if it is true, it means a great deal - there is very much involved in it. There may be activity in service, and liberality in the use of one's means, without any true devotedness.

By way of illustration, let us suppose that some Israelite had preferred to remain in Egypt at the time of the Exodus, and that he became very wealthy there. Let us suppose him to be professedly very anxious to serve the God of his fathers, and to honour the Lord with his substance; so much so that he devotes half his gains to Jehovah. He looks around on the misery of Egypt - he sees need and oppression on every hand - and he says to himself, What could please Jehovah better than to seek to ameliorate the condition of these wretched Egyptians? Jehovah is merciful and compassionate to all His creatures, and it must be pleasing to Him to do this good work. I will give half my goods to feed the poor, and to improve the condition of the submerged masses in Egypt, and by so doing I will honour the Lord with my substance. I have no doubt that such a man would have passed in Egypt as a very devoted man. But there would not have been an atom of true devotedness in him. He would have been in a totally false position, and the fact that he remained in Egypt would have been a deep dishonour to the Lord. His liberality and benevolence would have only served to emphasize the fact that he was in the wrong place - in a place where he could not have remained a single day if his heart had been right with God.

Let us suppose another case. An Israelite goes out of Egypt with his brethren, and remains with them until they come to a fertile oasis in the wilderness. Then he says to the others, You may go on to Canaan if you like, but this is the place for me. I don't want anything better than this, and I mean to stop here. So he builds his house and settles down there. After a few years we visit him, and we find that he has prospered. His family has increased, and two or three runaway Levites have joined him, and he has set up a little private altar for himself, and gives the fifth of his income to support the Levites and to provide sacrifices, etc. And he tells us that he desires to honour the Lord with his substance. This man would no doubt have a great reputation for devotedness among those who were ignorant of the true nature of Israel's calling. But everyone who knew Jehovah's purpose for His people would regard him as a man who despised the pleasant land, and who was dishonouring Jehovah by making light of His promises and purposes. If there had been true devotedness in him - if Jehovah had been really enshrined in his affections - he could never have settled down in such a place, and the first genuine bit of devotedness would move him to leave it altogether.

When the Lord is before our hearts we think first of His mind and pleasure, and it becomes our great concern to know what is on His heart for us, so that we may enter into it, and thus be in suitability to Himself and His thoughts. It was a suitable thing that the Israelite who was brought into the land and enriched with its fulness, should honour the Lord with his substance and with the firstfruits of all his increase. He was in possession of that which God's purpose and grace had bestowed upon him, and the Lord was well pleased to receive the firstfruits, which bore witness that he was in possession and enjoyment of the good land, and that he appreciated the grace which had brought him into it. It may be good for our hearts to consider where we are as to this elementary feature of true devotedness. Are we in Egypt, trying to do good there by helping all kinds of schemes for the betterment of man's condition in this world? Or are we in a little oasis of our own - carrying on worship and service after our own ideas? Or have we made it our great concern to apprehend the present thought and purpose of God for us? Are we really seeking to enter into and take possession of what He has given, so that we may bring the firstfruits of it to Him? God takes pleasure in our enjoyment and appreciation of that which it has been His great delight to give us.

It is in proportion as we apprehend the purpose of God, and take possession of the things which He has freely given to us, that we can, in a spiritual sense, honour the Lord with our substance. Alas! we are so ready to stop short of His purpose, and to settle down with something that meets our own ideas, without much exercise as to whether it is according to the mind of God. Many stay in Egypt and try to improve the world; many others settle down with an order of worship and service which is according to man in the flesh; while few, comparatively, are like Joshua and Caleb - set in their hearts to fully follow the Lord, and to enter into the purpose of His love.

"And with the firstfruits of all thine increase". The Lord loves to be honoured by that which is best and freshest in our souls. It is that which is fresh from the Lord that really honours Him. It is very sad to get into a religious rut, and pray and praise just as we have done for years. When a brother takes part in a meeting who has something fresh from the Lord - a fresh sense of divine love in his heart - it affects everybody, and the Lord is honoured thereby. If we have not got any fresh spiritual "substance" it is a thing we ought to be deeply exercised about; and if we have got spiritual prosperity, let us see that we honour the Lord with it. A sister who had been refreshed and helped at a meeting, might think of some other sister who had been hindered from getting there, and might carry to her what she had got for herself. I think that would be honouring the Lord with her increase.

Then, of course, devotedness will express itself in other ways. If the Lord be really in our affections we shall honour Him in our life, and by our lips, and by the use of our means. Whatever position we occupy, we shall therein "serve the Lord Christ", and seek to honour Him by the faithful and single-hearted discharge of our duty. We shall also count it a privilege to speak of Him as we have opportunity, and it is surprising how great is the sphere of individual service. We think it a considerable matter to get a few hundreds of men and women to attend a gospel preaching occasionally, but if one hundred Christians were each to speak of Christ to one soul a day for a year, more than thirty-six thousand persons would hear the gospel. I do not say this to underrate the importance of public preaching, but to give an idea of the large possibilities of individual work. And very often a little book may be given or sent by those who have small aptitude, it may be, for personal dealing with souls.

Lastly, if the Lord has His right place in our

hearts we shall honour Him with our substance in temporal things. Many saints are positively shrivelled up by a selfish and covetous spirit. They reap sparingly because they sow sparingly (2 Corinthians 9:6). If they give at all, it is because they feel obliged in conscience to do something, but they keep it within as narrow limits as possible. Others will spend money freely for their own gratification, and on things of no practical use whatever, while probably within reach of their own observation, if they had any eyes, some of the Lord's poor are lacking bread. Of such we may well ask John's question, "How dwelleth the love of God in him?" (1 John 3:17). Nor let the poor think they are excluded from this privilege of honouring the Lord with their substance. What are the brightest examples of this kind of devotedness in Scripture? Do we not read of a widow who had but a handful of meal and a cruse of oil, whose heart was so under the power of Jehovah's Name that she gave her all to His servant? Do we not read of another whose whole fortune consisted of "two mites which make a farthing", who "cast in all that she had, even all her living", into the treasury of Jehovah's house? Do we not read of another whose "substance" was but a box of ointment, that "she hath done what she could"? The greatest gifts, in God's account, are the gifts of the poor.

4. DISCIPLINE

"My son, despise not the chastening of the Lord; neither be weary of his correction: for whom the Lord loveth he correcteth, even as a father the son in whom he delighteth". This is a very distinct mark of wisdom's children, for it is written, "If ye be without chastisement, whereof all are partakers, then are ye bastards and not sons" (Hebrews 12:8). Everything that tries us, that is a check upon us, that causes exercise of heart, and makes us sensible of weakness in ourselves, is of the nature of chastisement. It may come in the way of difficulties in the path of faith; or in the shape of such trials and sorrows as are common to men - loss of property, loss of health, or bereavement; or it may be as the governmental consequences of sin; but in one way or other all have it. It is "for our profit, that we might be partakers of his holiness" (Hebrews 12:10). That is, it serves to break down that which is not of God in us, and thus it is a real help to us.

I cannot now go into the subject at any length, but I should like to call your attention to the twofold admonition in connection with it. The two things against which we are warned are Despising and Fainting. "Despise not thou the chastening of the Lord, nor *faint* when thou art rebuked of him" (Hebrews 12:5). To despise the chastening of the Lord is to treat it as if the Lord had nothing to do with it, as if it had happened purely by chance. Suppose I take cold and am laid aside by it, and I take it just as a matter of course - perhaps blaming myself for not being more careful - I think that is despising the chastening. It may be true that I was careless in exposing myself unnecessarily to a draught, and that as a natural consequence I took cold. But behind all that *the Lord* permitted it for my profit, and if I recognize the Lord's hand in it, and bow to His dealing with me, I shall get blessing out of it. It is wonderful what rest and peace one gets under the chastening when one recognizes *the Lord's* hand in it. The moment you turn to the Lord, and your heart says, I wonder what *the Lord* intends to teach me by this, the character of the chastening is altogether changed for you. Not that it is removed or altered, but it wears quite a different aspect to you. You own *the Lord's* hand in it, and then you are divinely exercised by it.

It is very common for believers to say, But my chastening is the result of my sin and folly. I am just reaping what I have sowed. How can there be any blessing in that? Well, my brother, if you have judged the sin and folly, and got right with the Lord about it all, you will be most ready to own His hand in the chastening. You will bow under it in subduedness of spirit, and humble yourself under the mighty hand of God, and such is His infinite grace that He will now make the consequences of your sin a great spiritual help to you. If the Lord's hand is in it, it is surely for your blessing. Then do not for a moment allow yourself to cherish the cold despairing thought that you are suffering under the action of an inflexible and mechanical law of nature. Your suffering is "the chastening *of the Lord*".

It seems to me that the Corinthians present to us an example of men who despised chastening. Many were weak and sickly among them, and many slept, and yet there does not appear to have been any recognition that this was the hand of the Lord. This shows that ministry may be used to enlighten us as to the object of chastening. Paul's epistle gave them light, and recovered them from the terrible condition into which they had fallen.

The second danger is that we may faint when we are rebuked of the Lord. The recognition of the Lord's *love* would preserve us from this. If we recognise the Lord in it, we shall not despise it; if we recognize His love in it, we shall not faint under it. "Whom the Lord loveth he correcteth". The consciousness that the chastening is all the outcome of divine love will preserve us from fainting. You have heard of the singer who went to a great master to be trained, and who, to his great surprise and disappointment, was kept singing one sheet of exercises for six years. Very weary did the pupil become of his exercises, but at the end of six years the master dismissed him as a perfect singer. The weary exercises had done their work in training and developing his voice, and all unknown to himself he had profited immensely by them. Many bitter hours of vexation would have been spared him if he had had unwavering confidence in the master's love. We, like him, have to go through our exercises, and often there is a sameness and monotony about them which makes the tendency to weariness very great. We are often inclined to think that the chastening is doing us no good, and that it is more a hindrance than a help. Beloved brethren, let us remember that a master hand has ordered those exercises for us, and deep eternal love is behind them all. How blessed to be able to look upon every trial and difficulty, upon every pressure and cause of exercise, as an express token of the Lord's love! We feel it to be "not joyous, but grievous"; it is a very real check upon us - it would not profit us if it were not; but we know the love that is behind it, and this is enough.

The Thessalonians give us an example of the liability to faint. The enemy seems to have used their tribulations and persecutions to discourage them, and to make them think that they were suffering in wrath from the Lord. The apostle writes to them to beseech them not to be "soon shaken in mind", or "troubled", and he speaks to them as "brethren beloved of the Lord", and prays that their hearts might be comforted by "our Lord Jesus Christ himself, and God, even our Father, *which hath loved us*, and hath given us everlasting consolation and good hope through grace" (2 Thessalonians 2:1,2; 2 Thessalonians 2:13; 2 Thessalonians 2:16,17). He seeks to confirm their hearts in the assurance of divine love, as the great preservative against the tendency to faint.

5. DILIGENCE

"Keep thy heart with all diligence; for out of it are the issues of life". The keeping of the heart answers to the "loins girded" of the New Testament. In a scene of evil and defilement our affections need to be held within the girdle of truth (Ephesians 6:14). This will not be needed in heaven; there will be no need for any restraint upon our affections there; but it is needed here. There is a constant tendency in our hearts to be attracted by things here, and when we come under their influence we are defiled. "Love not the world", says the Holy Ghost, "neither the things that are in the world. If any man love the world, the love of the Father is not in him. For all that is in the world, the lust of the flesh, and the lust of the eyes, and the pride of life, is not of the Father, but is of the world" (1 John 2:15, 16). It may be said that we cannot keep our hearts. Well, that is very true, and important to be known, but this scripture calls our attention to the responsibility side of the matter. For example, if I am earnestly praying to the Lord to keep my heart out of the world and for Himself, I should not think of getting a novel out of the Free Library to read, or of cultivating friendship with worldly people. If I am anxious to be "kept by the power of God", I shall certainly not fail to cleave unto the Lord "with purpose of heart". That all is of God's grace I fully own, but the way that grace works is by awakening and developing in us desire and purpose to "cleave unto the Lord". Satan is ever seeking to get something into our hearts that will divert us from Christ - that will draw us away from "first love". There is ever the necessity to keep our hearts "with all diligence". "Put away from thee a froward mouth, and perverse lips put far from thee". The lips have to be kept as well as the heart. In connection with our speech there are two great dangers. The man with the "froward mouth" will say what he thinks, or what he likes, without any consideration for others; and the man of "perverse (or inconsistent) lips" will say what he thinks will be agreeable to his listeners, and will sacrifice uprightness to his desire to please. One pregnant sentence from the New Testament furnishes a corrective for both. "Let your speech be alway with grace" - that will regulate the froward mouth - "seasoned with salt" - that will banish inconsistency and duplicity.

"Let thine eyes look right on, and let thine eyelids look straight before thee". There is a wonderful power of deliverance from present things in having an Object that commands the heart. Someone has said that a mother who heard that her child had been run over would not be diverted by the things in the shop windows as she went along. In Philippians 3 we see a man whose eyes looked right on - "I count all things but loss for the excellency of the knowledge of Christ Jesus my Lord: for whom I have suffered the loss of all things, and do count them but dung, that I may win Christ ... This one thing I do, forgetting those things which are behind, and reaching forth unto those things which are before, I press toward the mark for the prize of the high calling of God in Christ Jesus".

"Ponder the path of thy feet, and let all thy ways be established. Turn not to the right hand nor to the left: remove thy foot from evil". Wisdom's pathway is one of separation from evil. It is written, "Come out from among them, and be ye separate, saith the Lord, and touch not the unclean thing; and I will receive you, and will be a Father unto you, and ye shall be my sons and daughters, saith the Lord Almighty" (2 Corinthians 6:17, 18). And within the Christian profession the same principle is insisted upon, for we read, "Let every one that nameth the name of the Lord depart from iniquity" (2 Timothy 2:19). Many who would shun other kinds of iniquity are content to remain in association with religious evil. If you go on with that which you know to be contrary to the mind of God, how can you expect to have light or blessing from Him? You may, through His infinite grace, get a few crumbs of food and refreshing, but you cannot expect to have much light from God if you do not remove your foot from evil.

May each of us be characterized in a more distinct way by these marks of wisdom's children.

———————

STABILITY AND GROWTH
1 John 2

It should be clear to every Christian that there is such a thing as spiritual growth. In the scripture before us some of the children of God are addressed as "little children" or "babes", others as "young men", and others again as "fathers". In connection with this it should be noted that in verses 1, 12, 28 of chapter 2, and in verses 7, 18 of chapter 3, and in verse 4 of chapter 4 and in verse 21 of chapter 5 it should be simply "children". In these verses the whole of the children of God are addressed. But in 2: 13, 18 the word used is rightly translated "little children", and those addressed are the babes in the family.

Before the apostle addresses himself to the three different classes - babes, young men, and fathers - he states something that is common to all the children. "I write unto you, children, because your sins are forgiven you for his name's sake" (verse 12). Precious statement! True of all the children of God - of every believer on the Lord Jesus Christ! There is no growth as to this. It is as true of the youngest babe in Christ as it is of the oldest father. Let me ask, Are you in the blessedness of this great remission? When you say, "I believe in the forgiveness of sins", whose sins do you mean? Of course you believe that Peter, Paul, John, and the rest of the goodly fellowship of the apostles had their sins forgiven! But what benefit is this to you? You need the forgiveness of your sins. Can you say in the presence of God, My sins are all forgiven? It would be dreadful presumption for you to say this if it is not true. I advise you to be careful: it is an awful thing for a sinner to suppose that his sins are forgiven when they are not. But if God is proclaiming the remission of sins in the name of the Lord Jesus, and giving the assurance of pardon to all who believe, it must be because of indifference or unbelief if you cannot say that your sins are forgiven.

The Son of God - Jesus Christ the righteous - has been in the world to deal with sins. We could commit sins, but we could not put them away. A divine Person was needed to do that, and in love and grace He came to do it. "Jesus Christ the righteous ... is the propitiation for our sins: and not for ours only, but also for the whole world". Think of the mighty work accomplished when He "suffered for sins"! And for whose benefit was it accomplished? Were only the children of the promises to have title to this blood-bought pardon? Nay! the heart of God took in the whole world in thoughts of love and grace, and the atonement was equal to the mighty scope of that love and grace. "Not for ours only", says the apostle, "but also for the whole world". Oh! the divine greatness of that precious sin-atoning work!

Notice particularly how it is put. I think if we had written this we should have been likely to put it thus - "and he made propitiation for our sins", but that is not what the Holy Ghost says. The blessed Spirit wishes to concentrate our thoughts rather upon *the Person* who did the work than upon the work itself, and He says, "HE is the propitiation for our sins". All the value of the work resides in the Person who did it, and if you want to have the benefit of the work you must go to *Him* by faith - you must believe on His Name. A very simple illustration may help you to understand it. The medical student poring over his books, making his dissections, walking the hospitals, is working for his future practice. But when that work is done and he comes out as an M.D., all the value of the work resides in the person who has done it, and if you want the benefit of that long study and labour you must go to the person who did it. It is so in this matter of forgiveness. The great atoning work, which is its everlasting basis in righteousness, was finished - once for all - at Calvary; but all the value of that work resides today in the glorious Person who did it. "HE is the propitiation for our sins". Never, from the moment in which He cried, "It is finished!" to all eternity, can one jot or tittle be added to the perfection of His atoning work. All the efficacy and value of that work is available for every sinner under heaven, and is to be secured by faith in the Person who did it. The gospel proclamation is surely plain enough. Listen to it! "Be it known unto you therefore, men and brethren, that through this man is preached unto *you* the forgiveness of sins; and by him all that believe are justified from all things" (Acts 13:38, 39).

The Son of God, once here in the humiliation of matchless grace, once in death upon the cross to make atonement for sin, but now glorified at the right hand of God, is set forth on God's part as the propitiation for sins. And to every one who believes on His blessed Name it may be said, "Your sins are forgiven you for his Name's sake".

But this is not all. The forgiveness of sins does indeed settle every question connected with our responsible history as men and women in this world. It removes the burden of guilt from our consciences so that "we have peace with God through our Lord Jesus Christ", and great is the blessedness of this. But faith in Christ not only secures this for us, but it introduces us to an entirely new position and relationship. "As many as received him, to them gave he power to become the sons [children, it should be] of God, even to them that believe on his name" (John 1:12). Believers have the right to take the place of being children of God. The fact that they receive Christ by believing on His name, is the proof that they are born of God (see John 1:13). They are of kindred nature with God, and they receive and appreciate what is of God. A babe is not a very important personage in itself; everything depends on the family it is born into. Think how great it is to be a child in the family of God. Young believer, great is your dignity, and many are your privileges, because of the greatness of the position and relationship to which divine love has called you. We may well exclaim, "Behold, what manner of love the Father hath bestowed upon us, that we should be called the children of God" (1 John 3:1). The moral greatness of this infinitely surpasses every dignity that the world could confer. The apprehension of it makes the Christian bold to face contempt and rejection at the hands of men - makes him content to be despised and unknown by the world which "knew *him* not".

The first thing that is said of the "babes" is that they have "known the Father" (2: 13). In this we have the very essence of Christian blessing. "The Father" is the blessed Name in which God has revealed Himself in His beloved Son in all the fulness of infinite grace. There is nothing which enters more slowly into human hearts than the thought of grace. Indeed, many truly converted persons are very far from having reached the knowledge of the Father. We are, ofttimes, slow to believe that we may come by faith into all the privilege and joy of infinite grace without an atom of goodness, or merit of any kind, in ourselves. Then again, many seem thankful to hear of deliverance from death and judgment and of the remission of sins, but they do not seem interested in the grace from which all these blessings flow. Some may call it humility to be content with just that measure of blessing which will relieve the guilty conscience, and remove the fears of the soul, but it is really selfishness and indifference to grace. The prodigal in the far country may have thought it humility to ask to be made a hired servant in his father's house, but no such desire could escape his lips when the father fell on his neck and kissed him. It is the humility of faith to accept with joy and praise the fulness of blessing which grace delights to bestow. When the prodigal found himself seated at the father's table, robed, ringed, sandalled, and feasted, it could have been said to him, Thou hast known the Father. He had come into the circle of grace. His reception was altogether according to the father's heart, and in no wise according to his own deserts.

The moment we turn to God everything depends upon what God is, and the grace in which He receives us can only be measured by the Lord Jesus Christ, the risen and glorified One at His right hand. Nothing would suit the heart of God but that we should have the place and acceptance of sons before Him. He has marked us out for sonship "according to the good pleasure of his will, to the praise of the glory of his grace, wherein he hath made us accepted in the beloved" (Ephesians 1:5,

6). What a triumphant answer God has thus given to the slander of the serpent and to the unbelieving thoughts of fallen man! He has shown what He is in the blessedness of grace, that has undertaken to secure infinite blessing for man in spite of every obstacle which sin placed in the way. He loves to be known and trusted in this character, and the gospel makes Him known in this glory of grace. The babes know the Father - they know God in His infinite grace.

Then in verses 18-27 the babes are warned against the seductions of many antichrists. As to the world, it is "the last time". The manifestation of Christ has ended in His rejection, and the world has taken the character of antichrist. The coming of Christ - the Anointed and Holy One of God - into the world has brought out the true character of the world and its prince. The fact that God has revealed Himself in Christ, and set forth all His good pleasure in a Man in this world, has caused the power of darkness and evil to take the form of subtle - but definite and malignant - opposition to that blessed One. All this opposition will in a fast-approaching day find its head and centre in the personal antichrist, but "even now are there many antichrists". The principles which will characterize the personal antichrist are being spread abroad in a secret and seductive way by the "many antichrists", so as to divert men - and especially those who have had the light of Christianity - from the true knowledge of God.

The babes are warned against two forms of opposition to Christ - the denial that Jesus is the Christ, and the denial of the Father and the Son. The first is more especially the Jewish form of unbelief. Deluded by the father of lies, the Jews denied that Jesus was the Christ, and persist in that denial to this day. "The Christ" is the One in whom all the pleasure of God is found, and in whom is established every blessing for man. The denial that Jesus is the Christ is the effort of the enemy to divert men from Him as the One in whom God's pleasure and man's blessing are both fully established.

But in the denial of the Father and the Son lies the very essence of antichrist's work within the pale of Christianity. In Christendom it is not so much Satan's effort to represent Jesus as an imposter and blasphemer. The spirit of antichrist works in a more subtle way. Much is professedly made of Jesus as the greatest teacher and example the world has ever seen. He is held up as the desire of nations, and the ideal of humanity. But under cover of this the whole truth of Christianity - the revelation of the Father in the Son - is denied. Christ is made into the greatest of men, in order to rob Him of His personal glory as the Son of the Father. One must speak plainly as to this, for there is hardly any body of professing Christians today which is not largely imbued with the leaven of Unitarianism. Unitarians are often anxious to be called Christians, but they are really the unhappy dupes and tools of antichrist. In the apostles' days there was power in the Church, and fidelity to Christ, so that the antichrists could not remain amongst the saints. "They went out from us". It was from without that they attempted to carry on their evil work of seducing the babes. But in our days many of these antichrists are highly esteemed as teachers of Christianity, and the whole profession is more or less leavened by their influence.

Under such circumstances how are the babes to be preserved? To answer this question let us read verse 27, "But the anointing which ye have received of him abideth in you, and ye need not that any man teach you: but as the same anointing teacheth you of all things, and is truth, and is no lie, and even as it hath taught you, ye shall abide in him". The babes have received the Holy Ghost as a divine anointing that they may be taught of God, and they are thus divinely taught to find all truth in Christ the Son of God. The anointing abides in us, and ever teaches us to find all truth in the blessed Person of whom we have heard from the beginning, and thus, as we are divinely taught, we "abide in him". We find everything in Him, and we abide in Him. To leave Him would be to leave the truth and every blessing. We may well say, with Peter, "Lord, to whom shall we go? Thou hast the words of eternal life" (John 6:68).

The Holy Ghost will never teach us anything that is not set forth in Christ. He leads us on by unfolding that blessed One to our hearts in an ever-deepening fulness of grace and truth. If we have begun to know Christ, we have begun with that which will fill our eternity with blessedness and joy. Every earthly joy - even the sweet and holy joys of natural relationships and affections - will pass away, but the joy which our hearts have in Christ is eternal in its character - it is a bit of what will fill our eternity. Satan seeks to divert us by a thousand things which are "not after Christ" (Colossians 2:8), but the unction we have received from the Holy One ever teaches us to "abide in him". The fulness of the Godhead dwells in Him bodily, and it is our true blessedness to be filled full in Him who is the Head of all principality and power. The unction would turn our hearts to Christ with the same constancy as the magnetic influence turns the needle to the pole.

In John 14 we read, "The Comforter, which is the Holy Ghost, whom the Father will send in my name, he shall teach you all things, and bring all things to your remembrance, whatsoever I have said unto you" (verse 26). In John 15 we read, "When the Comforter is come, whom I will send unto you from the Father, even the Spirit of truth, which proceedeth from the Father, he shall testify of me" (verse 26). In

John 16 we read, "He will shew you things to come. He shall glorify me: for he shall receive of mine, and shall shew it unto you" (verse 13, 14). The Holy Ghost is thus the Remembrancer of Christ as He was here, the testifier of Christ as being now with the Father, and the unfolder of those "things to come" when everything in heaven and on earth will find its Centre in Christ according to the Father's counsels. Thus, whether the Spirit takes account of the past, the present, or the future, Christ is the substance of His ministry and the theme of His teaching. So that as we are taught by the unction which we have received, we "abide in him". May it indeed be so with each one of us!

One might know every verse in the Bible and yet be entirely unacquainted with the truth. It is not possible to acquire a knowledge of the truth by mental study of the letter of Scripture. The truth is presented in a Person, and it is as we know Him and abide in Him, that we know the truth. The Holy Ghost would make Christ everything to us. He comes to be in us as "the Spirit of the truth", so that the truth as set forth in Christ might dwell in us and be with us for ever (2 John 2).

I now pass on to say a few words about "the young men". They are addressed as being strong, and as having the Word of God abiding in them, and as having overcome the wicked one (1 John 2:14). If the "babe" be steadfast in the grace of God, and taught by the Spirit to abide in Christ as the One in whom all truth is set forth, he will soon be found possessed of the characteristics of the "young man". Being "strong" would result from knowing the Father; that is, it would be the effect of having the heart "established with grace". Then the effect of being taught by the unction to abide in Christ, as finding all truth set forth in Him, would be that the word, or testimony, of God would abide in the saints. Thus the efforts of the wicked one to seduce them would be frustrated. They would refuse to be diverted from Christ as The Truth, and they would continue in the Son and in the Father. They would overcome the wicked one. To such the solemn warning is addressed, "Love not the world, neither the things that are in the world. If any man love the world, the love of the Father is not in him. For all that is in the world, the lust of the flesh, and the lust of the eyes, and the pride of life, is not of the Father, but is of the world" (1 John 2:15, 16).

It is sometimes assumed that "babes" are in most danger of being drawn into the world and its things, but the Holy Ghost addresses this solemn warning to the "young men" and not to the "babes". The special effort of the enemy with the "babes" seems to be to corrupt them as to the truth - to divert them from grace, and from the knowledge of the Father and the Son - by what may be called religious error or false doctrine. But if his efforts are resisted, and the

Word of God gets an abiding place in the saints, he takes a different line. Many have been able to detect and resist false doctrine, who have afterwards been ensnared by the world. It is of all-importance that we should accept the warning here given, and also that we should see how saints are divinely preserved from the world and its things.

Let us consider for a moment what "the world" is. It is the whole system of things which has come into existence consequent upon the entrance of sin. A vast and complex system, in which everything can be found that ministers to the tastes, desires, and vanity of man as a fallen and sinful creature. There are three great types of the world in Scripture which answer to the three things that are in the world. Sodom is a type of the world as characterized by the lust of the flesh; Egypt represents it as marked by the lust of the eyes; and Babylon sets it forth as displaying the pride of life. In addition to these, I think Tyre and Sidon are typical of the commercial world, while "Jerusalem which now is" has become the symbol of the religious world. But as to their moral character, the commercial world and the religious world only present different phases of the three principles which are here said to be "all that is in the world".

"The lust of the flesh" refers to the baser and coarser appetites of men - sensuality, intemperance in eating or drinking, self-indulgence as to the body in every way. Indeed, it is pretty well summed up in what is said of Sodom. "Behold, this was the iniquity of thy sister Sodom, pride, fulness of bread, and abundance of idleness was in her and in her daughters, neither did she strengthen the hand of the poor and needy" (Ezekiel 16:49). It is still true that Satan finds mischief for idle hands to do, as David found to his cost (2 Samuel 11:1).

"The lust of the eyes" refers to self-indulgence in a more refined form. The eyes are figurative of intelligence, and there are an immense number of things in the world that afford gratification to the mind of man. Egypt is a type of the world in this aspect; we read of "the wisdom of the Egyptians". Science, literature, music, theatrical and other entertainments, present different forms of gratification suited to the tastes of different minds. It is by such things the "young men" are in danger of being ensnared. The heart may be drawn away by things which seem interesting and innocent in themselves. You do not "see any harm" in this or that? Perhaps not, but is it of the Father or of the world? Many things look very harmless, but their effect is to narrow the breach between your heart and the world, and to bring you nearer to men in the flesh. Perhaps nothing has done more to blight the souls of young Christians than the habit of reading fiction. Do you think you can retain spiritual health if you gratify the flesh by feeding on the very essence of the world, for this is what novels are? Religious novels are worse than the ordinary sort, for they connect divine things with unhealthy mental excitement.

"The pride of life" is that vainglorious lust which loves to be something in this world - to have a place and a name here. This lust will find its full expression in Babylon, where all the glory and magnificence of man and his works will come into display. Every ornate religious building and every lofty spire is a bit of Babylon. Men have taken up Christianity in name, but they do not desire to take up the reproach of Christ; so they have done their best to give Christianity greatness and glory in this world, so that the pride of man might have the fullest display under cover of the name of Christ.

Now how are we to be preserved from the world and its things? Verse 15 suggests the answer, for we read, "If any man love the world, the love of the Father is not in him". If the love of the Father is in us it becomes a divine preservative from the world. We are formed in, and become characterized by, the divine nature, whose holy tastes and desires find no gratification in the things of the world. The divine nature cannot be attracted by things which "are not of the Father". Our spiritual growth is not to be measured by our knowledge of Scripture, but by the degree of our formation in the divine nature. Scriptural intelligence is often far in advance of spiritual formation, and where this is the case there is great danger of the soul being ensnared by the world.

The babes have the knowledge of grace, but they have to grow in grace. The anointing has taught them to find all truth in Jesus Christ the Son of God, but they have to "abide in him". And "if that which ye have heard from the beginning shall remain in you, ye also shall continue in the Son, and in the Father". As we grow in the blessed grace of God, and abide in the Son of God, we are spiritually formed according to God. It is not only that we become more familiar with the letter and doctrine of things, but the truth forms our affections so that we are enlarged in our knowledge and appreciation of the Father and the Son. Thus coming up to the stature of "young men", we become capable of intelligent discernment, and we recognize that the world and its things are not of the Father. We do not need to go into the merits or demerits of things in detail. We have a judgment of the whole system, and of all that it contains. It is "not of the Father". Through grace we find our blessedness and joy in another system of things where everything is of the Father - things that have their eternal Centre in Christ glorified at the right hand of God. We cannot have both the things of the world and the things of the Father and the Son. There is no such thing as being half-and-half in this matter. "If any man love the world, the love of the Father is not in him".

Those who withstand the seductions of the many antichrists, and overcome the world, reach a third stage of spiritual growth. "I have written unto you, fathers, because ye have known him that is from the beginning". This is all he has to say to the "fathers", but it is infinitely blessed. They have found the rest and satisfaction of their hearts in the knowledge of Christ. The experience of Paul, as set forth in his letter to the Philippians, is that of a "father". Walking in self-judgment and in absolute distrust of the flesh, he had one Object before him. No seductive voice had been able to allure him from the light of heavenly grace which long years before had broken in upon him. The cross had become his cherished glory, as an impassable barrier between his heart and the world. Christ attracted and absorbed him. For Christ he had suffered the loss of all things, and counted the best things of earth but filth that Christ might be his gain. "That I may know him" was the pervading desire of his heart, and to be with and like Christ the goal to which he pressed on with unwavering purpose. He had "known him that is from the beginning", and his heart had found everything in that Blessed One. But was this only for an apostle? Surely not. It is instructive to note that he does not write in this epistle as an apostle, but as a servant of Jesus Christ (1:1). I am sure we are all perfectly conscious how small we are in comparison with Paul, and how far behind him in the race, but I trust many of us have our faces in the same direction. There is but one great Object in Christianity, and that is Jesus Christ, God's Son, the revealer of the Father. All spiritual growth is growth in the knowledge of Him. He is precious to the "babes", and as they abide in Him and grow up to the stature of "young men" they know Him better, but to the "fathers" He has become practically everything. May God graciously lead us on in the knowledge of Himself and His beloved Son, and give us grace to keep ourselves from idols!

———————

THE CROSS, THE HOLY GHOST, AND THE COMING OF THE LORD

Numbers 21:4-18

I wish to bring before you at this time three great landmarks of Christianity which we get in figure in this scripture. It is important to apprehend the scope of divine things. This enables us to judge things by the principles involved rather than by mere details. The three things to which I refer are the cross, the gift of the Spirit, and the coming of the Lord.

But before speaking of these things it may be helpful to glance at certain events in the previous history of the children of Israel. Thirty-eight years before, God had brought them out of Egypt that He might carry out His purpose of blessing according to the promises made to Abraham, Isaac, and Jacob. They were not redeemed because they were better than the Egyptians, for there was no difference in nature and practice between the Israelites and the Egyptians (see Ezekiel 20:5-9). Both alike deserved the judgment of God, but God wrought for His Name's sake, and in grace and sovereign mercy He put a division ("redemption", Exodus 8:23, margin) between His people and Pharaoh's people. It is God's grace and sovereign mercy that makes a difference between His called and chosen people and the world of the ungodly. But this could only be on the ground of atonement, and therefore the lamb must be slain and the blood sprinkled on every Israelite's doorpost and lintel. The Antitype of this is "Christ our passover ... sacrificed for us".

How could God in His holiness take us up on any other ground save that of atonement? "The precious blood of Christ" is of small account in the estimation of men, but it is of infinite value to God and to faith.

> *"Let one in his innocence glory,*
> *Another in works he has done;*
> *THY BLOOD is my claim and my title,*
> *Beside it, O Lord, I have none".*

Then, after being sheltered by the blood of the Lamb, the people had to learn the glorious power of Jehovah as a Saviour God. God is for His people against all the power of evil. On the ground of atonement God can claim His people for Himself, and act in victorious power on their behalf against every foe. So, at the Red Sea, they had to "stand still and see the salvation of the Lord". The divided waters, the dry land on which they passed through the Red Sea, the overshadowing cloud of Jehovah's presence, and the complete overthrow of the Egyptians in the midst of the sea, were all the blessed testimony of God's mighty power as a Saviour God. What answers to this for us can be found in Romans 4:24-5: 1.

Death is a place where man according to nature has no more footing than he has in the sea. But the fact that the Lord Jesus has come into death for us makes it "dry land" for those who believe. Faith now finds the surest footing in death, because He has died in the most blessed grace and love, that God might be known to us as a Saviour God. And now the hand that held up the watery walls of the Red Sea until the redeemed host had passed over, has raised up the Lord Jesus from the dead.

Believer, let this great fact enter your heart in all its amazing significance! The One who "was delivered for our offences", and who "his own self bare our sins in his own body on the tree", has been raised from the dead by the God whom He had so perfectly glorified. What a complete triumph of grace! And He was "raised again for our justification". He is the measure of our righteousness and acceptance with God. We may well sing that God has "triumphed gloriously!"

Consequent upon these wondrous actings of God in sovereign grace and mercy, the people found themselves in the wilderness. Canaan was their destiny and their inheritance according to God's purpose, but He led them forty years in the wilderness, as we read in Deuteronomy 8:2, to humble them, and to prove them, to know what was in their heart. There was, indeed, another side to the wilderness, for it was the place of divine resources and care, and where nature could only see a barren desert, faith saw God. But it was the place where the true character of the flesh came out.

The people had scarcely finished singing the song of redemption in Exodus 15 when it was manifested that they were still capable of murmuring against God. And all the way through the wilderness the flesh disclosed itself in many hideous forms. In the scripture we have read this evening the people are almost at the end of the wilderness, but the flesh is unchanged; they "spake against God, and against Moses".

Do we not know something of this? Have we not experienced the risings and rebellings of a nature that knows not how to submit to God's will? In the first joy of conversion we did not realize this; but since then many of us have had to learn that there was that in ourselves which was more terrible - more opposed to God - than we ever imagined before. We have had to learn the incorrigible badness of the flesh. "The carnal mind is enmity against God; for it is not subject to the law of God, neither indeed can be. So then they that are in the flesh cannot please God" (Romans 8:7, 8).

Death must come in upon what we are as in the flesh. "Much people of Israel died". It is not necessary that we should take literally forty years to learn that the flesh is incorrigibly bad, but we have to go through it in moral time, which is not measured by months and years, but by exercise of soul. It may be that Saul of Tarsus learned it in three days; others may never come to it until their death-bed. But the end reached is that we know "that in me, that is in my flesh, dwelleth no good thing". We are obliged to cry, "O wretched man that I am! who shall deliver me from this body of death?" (Romans 7:24).

It is at this point that we are prepared to understand the blessed import of the brazen serpent being lifted up. If we find ourselves full of the poison of sin, and therefore under death, it is clear that we must look for deliverance and life altogether outside ourselves. An object was lifted up before the eyes of the bitten Israelite, and by looking on that object he lived. Nothing could be more simple, yet nothing more profound and blessed.

The object that was lifted up had no poison in it, for it was made of brass, but it was made in the likeness of the creature that had the poison. As a type it answers to Romans 8:3. God sent His own Son in the likeness of sinful flesh, and He was lifted up as a sacrifice for sin. The One who knew no sin was made sin for us. He became sacrificially what we were actually, that He might remove sinful flesh from before God in holy judgment. I am not now speaking of sins, but of sinful flesh. I venture to say that many young believers are much more troubled by sinful flesh than by actual transgressions.

Very often when there is no outward act of sin the soul is sorely distressed by evil thoughts and fleshly desires and motives. These are the outcome of sinful flesh, and, being born again, you condemn not only the fruit but also the root from which it springs.

How blessed to see that sinful flesh has been condemned in the death of Christ! It was in boundless divine love and grace that He became a Sacrifice for sin. Nothing but His death could make an end of sinful flesh, but in that precious death it has been utterly condemned. Are you glad to know this? If you have not learned to hate yourself, you will not care to know the meaning of the cross. But if you have been harassed and troubled by sinful flesh until you abhor yourself, you will rejoice to know that it was condemned when the Son of Man was lifted up.

Thus the death of Christ is our title to be with God as those who are apart from the flesh. And not only has that precious death removed sinful flesh, but it has become to our wondering souls the revelation of God's grace and love. The death of Christ becomes our way out of death into life. It removes what we are, and it reveals what God is, so that we may find our blessedness and life in the knowledge of divine Persons.

But the love which was manifested in death still subsists in the Son of God risen and glorified, and by that love He binds us to Himself on the resurrection side of death. He says, "Because I live, ye shall live also". He has laid down His life for the sheep, that He might bring them into eternal life in association with Himself. As the glorified One, He gives eternal life to as many as the Father gives Him. All that constituted our life according to the flesh has been condemned in His death, that we might live in association with Him as risen from the dead. Is not this glorious beyond conception? We are called to participate in the life of the last Adam - to be associated with Him in His heavenly portion as the One who has gone to the Father. He came that we might have life, and that we might have it abundantly.

Then, after the lifting up of the brazen serpent, we come to the springing well - a God-given well which the princes and nobles digged while all Israel sang, "Spring up, O well!" In this we see a type of the Holy Ghost.

In John 3 we have the brazen serpent; in John 4 the springing well. "The water that I shall give him shall be in him a well of water springing up into everlasting life" (verse 14). We could not enter into eternal life except by the Spirit, for it is only by the Spirit that we can be superior to the flesh and its lusts. The man in Romans 7 is striving against sin, but it is too strong for him; he is weak and in bondage. In Romans 8:2 he is free. "The law of the Spirit of life in Christ Jesus hath made me free from the law of sin and death". A law is a principle which acts continuously in the same way, like the law of gravitation. The law of the Spirit of life in Christ Jesus makes free from the law of sin and death. The power of life is in the believer by the Spirit, and he thus becomes superior to the law of sin and death to which he was subject as in the flesh. He enters with God upon the new ground that he is in Christ Jesus, and he thus reaches power and liberty.

When the Lord speaks of the Holy Ghost as a well of water in the believer (John 4), it is evidently in connection with inward satisfaction. "Whosoever drinketh of the water that I shall give him shall never thirst", etc. The Holy Ghost is given to be a divine spring of refreshment and joy in the soul of the believer. He is given to carry our affections into a circle of things that death can never touch, and where we may find most blessed satisfaction in the knowledge of the Father and the Son. He is given to bring us into what has been called "a region of satisfied desire". Well may the murmurs of the wilderness give place in our hearts to the song, "Spring up, O well!"

Do we know anything of this, beloved brethren? Have we seen the end of the murmurer at the cross? Are we now in the power and joy of the springing well? It is one thing to know the doctrine as to these things, and another to realize the blessedness of the springing well in one's own experience. May God so attract us by these things that we may rejoice to part company with "our old man" at the cross, and that it may become our steady purpose to judge and renounce everything that would hinder the well from springing up in our souls!

Then, finally, they "pitched ... toward the sunrising", (Numbers 11:11). This is suggestive of the future. We might say that the cross is our past, the Holy Ghost is our present, and the coming of the Lord is our future. If we look around we see men making prodigious efforts to establish themselves in possession of the earth, and to subdue all the powers of nature to their service. But with all the boasted progress of science and education, dense moral darkness reigns here, for God is unknown. So long as the present state of things continues, every improvement, and every accession of knowledge, tends to exalt man, and more completely to exclude God. It is in the power of many now living to recall the effect of vast social improvements and marvellous inventions. Has not the effect been to make man more self-sufficient, and practically to exclude recognition of God from men's minds?

Is this state of things to continue indefinitely? No; God has set bounds to the pride of man, and in His appointed time He will set aside in judgment everything that is opposed to the knowledge of Himself. The Lord Jesus Christ is coming back in glory and power to subjugate everything to God - to overturn the whole present system of things - to dispossess the god and prince of this world - and to fill this very scene, where sin has displayed itself so long, with the knowledge and glory of God.

"All the proud, yea, and all that do wickedly, shall be stubble: and the day that cometh shall burn them up, saith the Lord of hosts, that it shall leave them neither root nor branch. But unto you that fear my name shall the Sun of righteousness arise with healing in his wings; and ye shall go forth, and grow up as calves of the stall" (Malachi 4:1, 2). Here we see the twofold effect of the coming of the Lord. All the pride and wickedness of man, which are so prominent now, will be burnt up, Everything that is prominent in the present system of things will be destroyed. Everything in which the glory of man appears will come to nothing. But, on the other hand, to those that fear God the Sun of righteousness will arise with healing in His wings. The oppression of the poor and needy will cease, the lowly will be exalted, and the meek will inherit the earth. The will of God will be done on earth as it is in heaven.

It is because the Christian looks for an entirely new order of things that he holds aloof from all the politics and schemes of the present age. He does not belong to the present age, and he cannot recognize it as being of God, He pitches toward the sunrising! All his hopes and expectations as to the ordering of things here are centred in the Lord Jesus Christ. He rejoices in hope of the glory of God. The Christian is sometimes regarded as being "behind the times", but in truth he is very much in advance of the times! Men are occupied with things which are going down - and going down under the judgment of God - but the Christian lives in view of a wonderful range of things which are coming up! The glory and blessedness of these things can only be known by knowing the Person who will bring them. It is the blessed Christ of God, who is now crowned with glory and honour at God's right hand, who is going to bring the glory of God into this poor, dark world. We know something of the excellence of what is coming by knowing Him. One might study prophecy a long time and yet have a very poor idea of the moral character of the age to come. But if we see the glory of God in the face of Jesus Christ, we are in the light of it all now. Not a ray of glory will ever shine out in the coming age that does not shine this minute in the face of Jesus Christ. So that in the light of that glory our hearts are removed from the empty glory of this present world, and we pitch "toward the sunrising". May it be so increasingly with each one of us!

———————

THE ACTIVE GRACE OF CHRIST RISEN

John 20:1-23; Luke 24:13-36

I am bringing before you some very familiar scriptures; indeed, they are so familiar that it is well if our very familiarity with them has not hindered us from realizing the importance and blessedness of that of which they speak. We have often been reminded that the first day of the week - the resurrection day - imparts its own peculiar character to Christianity; nor did it close without presenting in pattern the assembly - the saints gathered, the Spirit given, and the Lord in the midst.

My object in adverting now to this day is to bring briefly before you the activities of the Lord in resurrection. Does it not awaken at once a lively interest in our hearts when we ask, how was the blessed Lord engaged on that memorable day? We have often, it may be, meditated with profound delight on His activities in the days of His flesh. We have followed Him through the day of His activity as Jehovah's Servant on earth, from its sunrise at the baptismal waters of Jordan to its sunset in that awful hour of the power of darkness, when the night came of which He spake when He could no longer work. Blessed, indeed for us to know that the night did not overtake that peerless Servant until His work was done! I speak not - for the moment - of atonement, but of all those ceaseless activities of grace, in which He was the Servant of Jehovah's pleasure, and the Son of His Father's love as a Man upon the earth.

Then I trust every heart in this company has lingered with adoring thoughts of faith and love in presence of the work accomplished on the cross. There we see the One of whom we can say, through grace, that He is "all our salvation", accomplishing the work which gives Him title to be thus known by our poor hearts. There we see our sins and our whole state as children of Adam brought before God, and we see a divine Saviour under judgment and in death, that He might settle every question that sin had raised between God and our souls, and that He might so deliver us as to make Himself the object of our faith and the One in whom our hearts should find their every blessing and joy for ever.

But "the first day of the week" finds Him in a new condition. The "days of his flesh" ended; all His earthly associations with Israel and with men in the flesh entirely broken. He now comes forth in resurrection to be the Source and the Giver, and to present in His own Person the character of blessings altogether new. I am increasingly persuaded, my brethren, that the Holy Ghost would lead our heart's affections to that Risen One: and in order to this my present object is to bring before you His gracious activities as the Risen One. Have you thought of the round of service that occupied Him on that eventful day? We may truly say that it was a busy day for our blessed Lord.

A SORROWING HEART

His first action - and surely love would have it so - was to meet and satisfy the longings of a heart that had no object but Himself. A heart like Mary's had the first claim, we may say, on the attention of the Lord. And, beloved, to such a service as this His heart would joyously turn. His own precious words were - oh! that we may treasure them in our hearts - "He that loveth me shall be loved of my Father, and I will love him, and will manifest myself to Him" (John 14:21). With what delight did his eye rest upon that early visitor to His empty tomb! She loved Him, and her love called forth the expression of His. She wept for Him; she sought Him; she loved Him; and He loved her and manifested Himself unto her.

Now, beloved Christians, are our hearts turning from everything that is here because of the treasure we have in Himself? There is such a thing as turning from the world as philosophers and monks turn from it, in disgust, when it has disappointed and vexed us, or when our power to enjoy its things is gone, or in a religious way to build up a religious character for ourselves. But the Lord looks for something different from this. He looks - yes, He is looking now - for the heart that longs after Himself. Has the treasure we have found in His love really separated our hearts from everything here?

I do not ask whether you understand church truth, or dispensational truth, or resurrection truth. You might know a great deal about these things and yet be like the disciples of whom we read in John 20:8-10. They saw. Yes! it was as clear as noonday that the Lord was risen. They believed, too, that He was risen. But though the intelligence was right and the faith was right, there was something else which was singularly wanting - perhaps I ought to say dormant. Can you understand the lack of that wanting element? Have you no key to it in your own experience, which compels you now to own in your conscience that their condition is but a picture of your own? Indeed, my brethren, we see many things clearly enough; we can perhaps define them with mathematical accuracy; in a certain way we believe them; and yet our practical everyday life is but little affected thereby. We still live in the narrow, selfish circle of our own things and our own interests. "The disciples went away again unto their own home".

It was far different with Mary. Hers was a widowed heart. The sunshine of her life had gone. As someone has said, all the world was a blank to her because He was gone. Neither apostles nor angels could fill the void in that bereaved heart. Christ had made Himself everything to her; with Him she had all, without Him she had nothing. It is easy to speak with cold criticism of her lack of intelligence; but, my brethren, it might be well for some of us if we could part with some of our intelligence, and receive in exchange a little more of that whole-hearted and self-forgetting affection for Christ, which made her homeless and without an object in the world where He was not.

It was to a heart like hers that the Lord delighted to manifest Himself. A single word sufficed to dispel the sorrow of that broken heart, and to fill it with immeasurable satisfaction and delight. It was that one word "Mary". It was not any communication made. It was nothing but Himself, and the consciousness of His presence and love borne into her heart, as the well-known Shepherd's voice called His sheep by name. Divine communications of the most wonderful nature followed, but there must be a suited condition of heart to receive divine communications, and that condition of heart was found in Mary. That one word from His lips filled and satisfied her heart. She had reached Himself, and that was everything. It was to a heart like that the blessed Lord could make communications which surpass all human thought - to such a heart He could unfold what divine love would do for its own delight in the blessing of its objects.

Her love would have kept Him here, and been content to follow Him still as the Messiah upon earth; rejected and dishonoured indeed, but still to her the chiefest among ten thousand and altogether lovely. But His love had its own secrets, and He tenderly set aside her thoughts that He might replace them by His own. "Touch me not, for I am not yet ascended to my Father", His death had proved there was nothing for Him here, but it had also proved that there was nothing for Mary here. Now He leads her heart to *a new world* by telling her that He is going there. She had known Him here and lost Him; now He reveals Himself to her in connection with a scene where nothing can ever break the link with Himself. He is going to His Father, but He is going as the "Leader of a chosen race". He has those in this world whom He owns as His brethren - His Father is their Father, and His God is their God, and His love would have them to know this new place of association with Himself as the risen One. What a revelation to the sorrowing heart that yearned after Himself! She had found Him in resurrection, in a new condition where the links could never be broken, and she had learned that she was one of a company whom He owned as His brethren - all of one with Himself. Every longing in her heart was more than satisfied. Beloved brethren, is it so with ourselves? If not, depend upon it we have not really taken in the thoughts of His love, and it may be the Lord has not found in us that freshness of affection for Himself that would set Him free to communicate those thoughts to us.

A SOILED CONSCIENCE

But it is not with all as it was with Mary. Alas! how few there are whose hearts are wholly absorbed by Christ! There are many whose hearts are not free because their consciences are burdened. They are not right with the Lord. They are under a cloud. They can say -

"What, happy hours I once enjoyed,
How sweet their memory still!"

But their spiritual joy has fled. Instead of holy thirstings after Christ, and the joy of His love, there is nothing in their soul's secret history but sadness and reproach. How is it? In some way the flesh has been allowed, the Spirit has been grieved, and the Lord dishonoured. The conscience is soiled, and the matter has never been bottomed with the Lord. On that resurrection day, while Mary's heart was being made glad as we have seen, there was another disciple who was under a cloud. Poor Peter! Who can tell the agony of that fervent spirit since the hour when the Lord turned and looked upon him, and he went out and wept bitterly?

I may here remark that there are two things to which almost every fall can be traced. One is spiritual indolence, and the other self-confidence. David is an example of one, and Peter of the other. It was the time "when kings go forth to battle"; why then was David tarrying at Jerusalem? a pernicious indolence clogged his footsteps, and you know the consequences. No doubt the palace royal was more congenial to flesh and blood than the battle-field, but tarrying there threw David into temptation he would never have had if with purpose of heart he had been acting as a king. If the Lord has called you to any service and you neglect it, you are sure to get into trouble. Lot is another example of spiritual indolence. The mountain life, with its daily exercises and its constant demand for the energy of faith, was too laborious for him. His eye rested upon well-watered plains. The dwellings of Sodom seemed more secure than the mountain tent, and he went down to the city whose sin was "pride, fulness of bread, and abundance of idleness". You may shrink from the troubles of faith, but if you shirk them you will have the troubles of sin, which are much worse to bear. If you look back to see where you have dishonoured the Lord, I think you will see that it was when you had been neglecting the Word of God and private prayer, and your heart was not going diligently after the things of the Lord.

In Peter we see self-confidence. He loved the

Lord, and he was confident in the strength of his love, and he needed to learn what a bruised reed he was. He did learn it, as we know, in a most humiliating way, and bitter was the lesson to his soul. Who can tell what scalding tears coursed down his cheeks! and what bitter self-reproaches he heaped upon himself! But was he forgotten by the Lord? Nay! Mark 16:7 reveals a precious touch of grace: "tell his disciples and Peter". Why should Peter be specially mentioned? Would it not have been enough to have said "his disciples?" Ah! Peter might have said, I cannot call myself a disciple any longer. I have denied Him. Such a name is not for me. So it must needs be that Peter has special mention. Then, furthermore, Luke 24:34 tells us of the Lord's second appearance in resurrection, "The Lord is risen indeed, and hath appeared to Simon". We know not what passed at that private interview, but I will venture to say that there was so much confession on Simon's part, and so much tender and gracious love on the Lord's part, that when the Lord and Simon met again, within the closed doors in the evening, no uneasiness or shyness remained to hinder Simon from enjoying the presence of his Lord.

If there is a Peter here tonight - one who has failed, and dishonoured the Lord - I can tell you that that dishonoured Lord loves you still, and it would give His heart great joy to remove the soil from your conscience and to make you happy in His love. Is there a shadow between your heart and Himself? Has something been allowed to get in, so that instead of being happy with the Lord you are ill at ease? You feel that there is a reserve, and you are reluctant to go straight to Him and to have it all out. The Lord would have that reserve to be banished from your heart, and this is the great object of His present dealings with you. He makes you conscious of your sin, but He does not fail to assure your heart of the constancy of His love. Look at all those links in the chain of His gracious dealings with Peter: (1) the prayer, Luke 22:32; (2) the warning, verse 34; (3) the counsel, verse 46; (4) the look, verse 61, (5) the message, Mark 16:7; (6) the private interview, Luke 24:34; (7) the full restoration, John 21:15 - 17. Every link bears the stamp of divine and changeless love. The Lord would not rest until He had His poor disciple alone with Himself to have it all out. It is to this end that He is speaking to you. Satan would keep you away from Him, and use the failure to create and widen a breach between you and the Lord. The active grace of the Lord comes after you now, as it went after Peter, that the breach may be completely healed. Get alone with Him and have it all out. Make a clean breast of the whole matter; go to the very bottom of it with Him; and you will find that He will remove the shade from your heart and the stain from your conscience, and give you a deeper sense of His love than you ever had before.

But the risen One has now before Him another service. He first satisfies a sorrowing heart; then relieves a soiled conscience; and then He has to think of

STRAYING FEET

Mark how the Holy Ghost introduces the subject! "And, behold, two of them went that same day to a village called Emmaüs". It is as though the Holy Ghost marvelled at such a thing. They were true disciples - they loved the Lord - they were not happy in going away - they had heard that He was alive - and yet they went! While He was with them He kept them, as He said; but now that He was gone and nothing remained for sight, they sorrowfully decided that the best thing they could do was to go back, as I suppose, to their own home.

We may be under influences of a natural kind which keep us outwardly right, without being at all in the faith of God's purpose. Then when the influences are removed we drift back to our own things. How often we see saints whose feet are kept right so long as certain influences are acting on them, who turn into a wrong path as soon as those influences are removed. I do not mean going into sin, as men speak, but going back to think only of their own things. It was so with Paul's converts. When he was put in prison he had to say that all in Asia had turned away from him, and that all were seeking their own things and not the things which were Jesus Christ's.

The fact was that the two whose course we are now considering were disappointed. Things had not turned out as they expected. Disappointment is a fruitful source of backsliding. Then let us be quite sure that our expectations are according to God's purposes. If we expect on the line of God's purpose we shall never be disappointed. These two had been looking for earthly blessing in connection with a living Messiah, and when all hope of this had been withered by His death they were sad and disheartened. Their expectations were on a wrong line, and the blessed Lord goes after them and speaks to their hearts that He might lead them on to the line of God's purposes in resurrection. Think of Him, just risen from the dead, walking eight miles with those two wanderers that He might conduct their hearts into the wonderful secret that God was going to establish everything in resurrection.

In short, He was leading their hearts to Himself in that new and "out of the world" condition into which He had entered as the Risen One. With what surprised burnings of the heart did they hear of the wonderful change in God's programme, which even Old Testament scriptures had announced beforehand. As their feet paced the road to Emmaüs their hearts and minds were being conducted by the wondrous stranger along a moral road which ended in the revelation of Himself in resurrection.

Do not let us suppose that the journey is one which only they needed to take. It is equally necessary and important for ourselves. It is so easy and natural for our hearts to connect the blessings of God with ourselves as men in the flesh, instead of seeing that the blight of death is upon everything that is of that order. We have to learn that all the blessings of God's present grace are wrapped up in One who is risen from the dead, and in order to reach them and have the joy of them we must reach *Him* who is no longer to be known after the flesh. If all expectation of blessings of a natural order is blighted by His death, He reveals Himself in resurrection as the source of infinite blessings of a spiritual order. When at length He made Himself known as the Risen One to the two disciples, it dawned upon their hearts that there was a new order of blessing infinitely surpassing all the earthly blessings for which they had been looking. Instinctively they turned at once to seek the company of their brethren. His death had broken all the earthly links that had held them together, and had put them outside everything that was recognized by men; but now His resurrection had put a new complexion upon everything, and they hastened to be found with the company which had been gathered, as someone has beautifully said, by the message sent by the risen One to His brethren. His gracious service had accomplished its end.

Thus, at the close of that memorable day, were the brethren gathered together. Gathered upon the new ground that Christ was risen, and gathered as the "brethren" of the risen One, He could have His own joy in being in their midst. I do not enter now into the wonderful character of that gathered company. You may perhaps feebly conceive what it was to Mary, to Peter, and to the two disciples of Emmaüs to know the Lord in His new condition as the Risen One, and to be found in a company to whom He could manifest Himself! But what was it for Him to gather His own company thus for the first time around Himself as the risen One! In the midst of that company His heart could let itself freely out. HE was in the peace of accomplished redemption, for all the judgment of sin was fully borne; God was glorified; His work was finished; the storm that had bowed His blessed head was hushed for ever. He was now in cloudless peace, but it was peace which He could share with this gathered company. He could impart to them the same peace that He was in as the risen One. Then if *He* had been quickened out of death by the Spirit, He would associate this gathered company with Himself in life, breathing upon them the Spirit of life. To that company He could declare the Father's Name; in their midst He could sing praise to God; and He could entrust to them the maintenance of His interests and glory, as the Father's interest and glory had been entrusted to Him. It was a company gathered *by* and *for* Himself; His own company, or, as He says in Matthew 16 - "*my* assembly".

May we better understand that it is the purpose of His love to have us here for Himself, and that all the wonderful grace that meets us in our need - whether it be that of the sorrowing heart, the soiled conscience or the straying feet - is bent upon dealing with us in such a way as to free us for Himself and for His own company! may we know truly what it is to be gathered together to His Name!

———————

REMNANT CHARACTERISTICS

Brief notes on an address on
Zephaniah 3:11-20

These verses describe the character of the faithful remnant of God's earthly people just before the kingdom glory dawns on this poor world. They show us the spirit that befits the remnant in the moment before the glory.

"I will take away out of the midst of thee them that rejoice in thy pride; and thou shalt no more be haughty because of mine holy mountain". The most fearful display of man's pride is when he takes the tokens of God's favour and plumes himself with them. The natural man always has his own glory before him; self is always his centre; and it is very easy for us to drift in that direction. When once we are born of God we can never go back and become natural men, but we may get as far as being carnal men. The saints at Corinth were carnal; they were setting themselves off with their divine gifts. Like those of whom this verse speaks, they were haughty because of God's favour to them. Remember, beloved, there is such a thing as spiritual pride. Let us beware of haughtiness in divine things.

"I will also leave in the midst of thee an afflicted and poor people, and they shall trust in the name of the Lord". The remnant has no place or influence in the world; it is composed of those who are nobodies here. They are like Him who was poor in spirit and never asserted His rights. They have a "little strength", but they keep His word, and do not deny His name. In their weakness they trust in the name of the Lord. Oh! that the Lord would draw our hearts away from everything to Himself.

"The remnant of Israel shall not do iniquity, nor speak lies". The next characteristics of the remnant are holiness and truth. The blessed Lord presents Himself to Philadelphia as "He that is holy, he that is true", and the overcomer takes his character from Him. Holiness is a great topic amongst Christians at the present day, and all kinds of methods are adopted for its promotion. I should like to impress upon you that there is no true Christian holiness that does not take its character from the Lord Jesus Christ *in the place where He now is*. There may be a great deal of religiousness without true holiness. The wonderful fact is that there is a Man not only separated from sin, but from sinners. That is, He is out of the scene of sin altogether, and in a scene where everything is suited to God and everything reflects the mind and purpose of God. He is there to be the Object of our hearts, and thus to take our minds and affections out of this scene where sin has desolated everything, into that scene where sin can never come. May

God's Spirit write it on our hearts that true holiness takes its character from that blessed One at the Father's right hand. "Every one that hath this hope in him purifieth himself, even as he is pure".

"They shall feed and lie down, and none shall make them afraid". Satisfaction and tranquillity are the next marks of the remnant. You can never have the second without the first. In the first half of Psalm 23 the soul is satisfied as to all its needs and desires; in the second half it is tranquillized in the presence of all the power of evil. The Lord is a Sun to light up our hearts with divine satisfaction, and then He is a shield to defend us from all our foes. "The Lord is my light and my salvation; whom shall I fear?"

"Sing, O daughter of Zion; shout, O Israel; be glad and rejoice with all the heart, O daughter of Jerusalem". If we have lost our old portion and our old joys, we have a new portion and new joys. Oh! that we knew the new joys as well, and pursued them as earnestly, as we once did the old joys! The old joy was like the crackling of thorns under a pot; like a strain of music that holds the ear for a moment and then dies for ever away. How different the joy that is in the Lord! Paul and Silas, when their backs were smarting and their feet were fast in the stocks, could sing aloud in their joy. The prisoners heard them singing praises to God. It was the new joy, and the circumstances never touched it. I can fancy the Philippian jailor reading that verse, "Rejoice in the Lord alway: and again I say, Rejoice", and understanding it a good deal better than we do.

"The Lord hath taken away thy judgments, he hath cast out thine enemy". He has removed everything, by His work, that would hinder our peace or joy. If you are not happy it is because you are allowing or bringing back something which Christ died to put away.

"The Lord in the midst of thee". Do we really know what it is to be in His company? We believe Matthew 18:20, but have we proved it? An old woman had her Bible marked opposite certain texts with the letters "T" and "P". The minister saw them, and asked what they meant. "Oh!" she said, "it means TRIED and PROVED". Have we proved the great reality of the Lord's presence in the midst of His gathered ones? Nothing can imitate it; nothing can be a substitute for it. I am sure, if we knew the reality of it, it would not be a little thing that would keep us away from the assembly, and we should go with much self-judgment for fear that anything should unfit us to taste the joy of His company.

"In that day it shall be said to Jerusalem, Fear thou not: and to Zion, Let not thine hands be slack". If we have done with the energy and restlessness of the flesh, let us beware that we do not fall into the sluggishness and indolence of the flesh. Are we like the men of purpose in Gideon's host, who would snatch the water and press on to the battle? Are we here in real spiritual energy for Christ! Or are we like the great majority who were content to take it easy and to consider their own comfort first? We once did evil "with both hands earnestly": shame on us if our hands are slack in the interests of Christ!

"The Lord thy God in the midst of thee is mighty". What a blessed word for our hearts today! To Philadelphia He presents Himself as the One who has the key of David, who opens and no man shuts, and shuts and no man opens. He is *mighty* if we have but a "little strength". What we need is to have more confidence in the power of our Lord Jesus Christ. There is a day coming in which He will exercise His power in government, and everything in the vast domain of creation will be set right. He is exercising that power now in grace, in and for the assembly. If we believed it, should we look to any other source for power? Impossible. "He will rest in his love; he will joy over thee with singing". He can rest in what His own love has accomplished. He has made us everything that His heart longed for, and now He has His joy in us.

Is there anything more? Yes, He desires one thing more. "I will make you a name and a praise among all people of the earth". He will display us to wondering worlds as the objects of His love. To Philadelphia He says, "I will make them to know that I have loved thee". May His words thrill our hearts tonight, "Behold, I come quickly: hold that fast which thou hast, that no man take thy crown". We are just on the eve of His coming; the last grains of sand are fast running out. People talk about prophetic periods - the only prophetic period for us is the twinkling of an eye.

———————

AFFECTION FOR CHRIST:
ITS AWAKENING, DECLINE AND REVIVAL
2 Corinthians 11:1-3

The subject which is before me tonight, is that of affection for Christ, or the state of heart which the Spirit is here to produce in the saints, and by which they answer to the present thoughts of Christ. I am afraid that when we speak of being *here for Christ* it is often the thought of our service or conduct that is prominent, and therefore it is well to be reminded that there is something over which Christ is more jealous than He is over our conduct or our service. It is that "garden enclosed", that "spring shut up", that "fountain sealed", from which all others but Himself are excluded - the hidden spring of those affections which alone satisfy His heart, or render conduct and service acceptable to Him.

This is very strikingly expressed in the words which we have just read, where we see the object of the true evangelist. He is a man bent upon *a present result for Christ*. He is not anxious to have a number of converts whom he can count as his own; he is not thinking of himself, but of his Master; he is wanting those whom he can present "as a chaste virgin to Christ". It is not that he loses sight of the eternal result, but the immediate object on which his heart is set, and for which he longs with intense fervency, is a present result in a people whose affections are altogether for Christ. "I have espoused you to one husband, that I may present you as a chaste virgin to Christ".

This is a great object before the heart of God at the present time - to have a people saved not only from judgment and the lake of fire, but from the world; saved not only for heaven by-and-by, but for the heart of Christ now. The work of Christ on the cross has settled every question that sin raised between God and our souls, and the future is bright with the glory of God, into which we shall be brought according to all the value of that work. But there is another thing, and that is the interval between the cross and the glory - an interval marked, so far as this world is concerned, by the dishonour and rejection of Christ. Satan cannot touch the value of the work of the cross, nor can he mar the perfection of the eternal glory, but the whole force of his power is put forth to hinder a present result for Christ. On the other hand, all the energy of the Holy Ghost is active to produce a present result for Christ. Every believer is looking to be to the satisfaction and joy of Christ in the eternal future; and surely none of us would like to say that we did not care whether we were to His satisfaction now or not, and yet, alas! *practically* it very often comes to this.

I think a verse from Jeremiah 2 may help us to see in an Old Testament type when the soul may be looked upon as espoused unto Christ. "Thus saith the Lord, I remember thee, the kindness of thy youth, the love of thine espousals, when thou wentest after me in the wilderness, in a land that was not sown. Israel was holiness unto the Lord, and the firstfruits of his increase". I have no doubt that these words refer to the time when the children of Israel were brought through the Red Sea. They were brought into the joy of complete deliverance from the power of the oppressor and from the land of judgment. Jehovah Himself became everything to them - their strength, their song, and their salvation; His victory and glory, and His thoughts and purposes, filled their hearts. They were absorbed with Himself. Read the song, Exodus 15. It is all "Thou", "Thy", "Thee", "Thine"; if they speak of themselves it is as "Thy people". It was a wonderful moment. You may say that it did not last long. That is true; but think of the wonderful blessedness of it while it did last. It was what Jehovah could remember and speak of more than eight hundred years afterwards as "the kindness of thy youth, the love of thine espousals".

Such a moment as that has come in the history of every soul who knows the salvation of God. Perhaps it was some time after you were converted; you may have been under the shelter of the blood for years before you came to it; but there is a moment - never to be forgotten - when Christ risen comes before the soul, and the greatness of His victory, and the share we have in it, and the wonderful purposes of God for us - all secured by that victory - take possession of the heart. We are brought to One who has been raised again for our justification, and through Him we find ourselves clear of the judgment land and the oppressor's power. There is no sense of need in the soul that is in the presence of Christ risen; there is a sense of boundless favour, for the soul is conscious (though it might not know how to explain it) that we share in the victory as belonging to the One who has won it. Through Him we have access into favour. But the soul who has come to this is not thinking so much of the favour or blessing as a thing in itself, but as that which we have in connection with Him, and as belonging to Him. If I belong to Him, the more wonderful His victory and position the more wonderful mine is, but I think of it all as His. I do not think that we rightly get a sense of belonging to Him until we come to Him as the Risen One, but I believe every heart that knows Him as risen from the dead has the consciousness, I belong to Him. I believe Thomas had it when he said, "My Lord and my God". I am not speaking of knowing truths or doctrines at all, but of a consciousness in the soul that has really reached Christ risen. I believe that to be the moment of the soul's espousal unto Christ. There may be much to learn, but there is great affection for Christ. All the wealth and wisdom of Egypt would not have tempted back at that moment those who sang the song, "Israel was holiness unto Jehovah".

No doubt there are many believers who have not reached a Risen Christ, simply because they have not had a Paul to "espouse" them to that "one husband". They have not heard of His glorious victory, or of His new place as the Risen One; they are struggling on in Egypt's darkness and bondage; their lives are being wasted in worldly thoughts and upon worldly things, and in many cases they do not know but that they are doing God's service - going in for politics and temperance and so on - trying to make Egypt better, instead of seeing that the whole scene is under the enemy's power and the judgment of God. If believers knew that the whole system of the world was under the leadership of Satan and the judgment of God, they would be heartily glad to be clear of it all. But how few there are to proclaim that the world is a judged thing before God, and that Christ and all the blessings of Christianity can only be found on the platform of resurrection. How few there are in Christendom today who are really seeking to bring souls to a Risen Christ - to espouse them to one Husband, that they may be presented as a chaste virgin to Christ.

I trust many of you understand the blessedness

of a moment when Christ is really known by the heart outside everything here in the infinite greatness of His own triumph, and you are conscious that you share in it all because you belong to Him. I venture to say that at such a moment the offer of £21,000 a year would have very little power to attract your heart. You had found a Person outside everything here, who was infinitely more to your heart than all the things of earth. You had stepped on to the shore of a new world, and found yourself supremely happy there, and the old world was totally eclipsed and superseded. It was the kindness of your youth and the love of your espousals. There was One whom, not having seen, ye loved, and in whom, though ye saw Him not, yet believing, ye rejoiced with joy unspeakable and full of glory. The vain things that had charmed you were forgotten or only remembered with shame, and you gladly accepted a part in the rejection of Christ here, because of the satisfaction you had found in Him on the other side. I trust many of you have known the reality of such a moment in your history. Now that is the true beginning of a Christian, and the Spirit of God is jealous over us that these affections should be maintained in freshness and fervency in our souls. It is thus - and only thus - that Christ has His true satisfaction in us, for if the day of espousal yields deep and holy joy to us, it yields a deeper and a fuller joy to Him, whose matchless love has drawn forth the responsive affection of our hearts. It is "the day of his espousals, the day of the gladness of his heart" (Song of Songs 3:11).

We can easily understand that if the devil has succeeded in turning Christ out of this world, it will be no pleasure to him to see a people here to whose hearts Christ is everything. Therefore it is his great object to corrupt our minds from simplicity as to the Christ; and this he seeks to accomplish, not by an open attack upon Christ, but "as the serpent beguiled Eve through his subtlety". He had introduced amongst the saints at Corinth men who pretended to be the apostles of Christ, and had all the appearance of ministers of righteousness (2 Corinthians 11:12-15). These men were going about amongst the saints discrediting Paul, and under a great show of doing the Lord's work they were craftily bringing in fleshly and worldly principles, and so far as they were accepted and tolerated, the saints' minds were corrupted from simplicity as to the Christ. I daresay they were careful not to assail what we call foundation truths. The devil knows better than to put in the thick end of the wedge first. It would not do for them to show their colours openly at first; but everything would be modified, and more or less humanized, and stripped of its proper force and bearing.

I am sure this is of great importance to us all, for I think we should all be prepared to admit that there is a great lack of the simplicity of affection to which Christ in resurrection is everything. The question arises, why is it so? Why do saints who have known what it was to be espoused unto Christ get so cold in their affections? How are they brought to be satisfied and comfortable again in worldly and carnal things? I do not believe that any person who had known what it was to be espoused unto Christ would go in for worldliness, until his mind had been corrupted by something that lessened his judgment as to what the world is. Before the outward departure, the corrupting influence is at work within; the mind is being occupied and permeated with thoughts and principles that connect themselves with man and with things here, and all this is done in such a subtle way that very often no alarm is felt in the conscience during the process. It is a solemn thing to say, but I believe that the decline of affection for Christ, and the corrupting process which precedes that decline, can often be traced to the influence of ministry that is not on the line or in the current of the Spirit of God. I think the chapter before us shows plainly that there are two kinds of ministry - the true and the false - that which is of Christ and the Spirit, and that which is of Satan - the one flatly opposed in its tendency and effect to the other. All true ministry in the power of the Spirit tends to draw our hearts away from man and from things here to Christ in resurrection.

False ministry occupies us with man and with things here, and hence draws our hearts away from Christ, for He can only be known as outside everything here, in resurrection. I am speaking soberly and in sorrow when I say that the overwhelming preponderance of ministry at the present day is of the latter character. It is inevitably so when the minister himself is unconverted, or has never known for himself what it is to be espoused unto Christ; but we must not overlook the fact that a man may be converted, and may know a good deal of truth, and yet the general drift of his ministry may be to occupy souls with things on this side of resurrection. Men may have the reputation of great piety, and they may say much that is good and true, and yet the real tendency of it all may be to occupy you with man and with things here. You know as a matter of fact that to be a good citizen, and to take part in everything that is supposed to tend to the improvement of the world, is looked upon by many even evangelical believers at the present day as a part of Christianity; and all the great religious bodies are more or less occupied in seeking to improve their position and enlarge their influence in this world. Woe betide us if we are drawn into this current. True affection for Christ is completely blighted thereby, for He can only be known in resurrection, and as One utterly rejected by man.

We cannot be too careful as to the influences

which we allow to act upon us. We are affected by all that we hear and by all that we read - unconsciously it may be. The damage is done before we know it; like Ephraim, we have grey hairs and know it not. I do not think you can put yourself under the influence of the ministry which is generally found even amongst evangelical Christians at the present day, either by hearing or reading it, without suffering loss in your soul. You will find your heart turned back to things here - perhaps religious things - and correspondingly brought away from Christ in resurrection.

I need not say that worldly literature of all kinds has the same effect. I am quite sure that a man cannot soak his mind in a newspaper every morning and retain freshness of affection for Christ. Of course a man in business may have to look at the market price of timber, or stone, or corn, just as a Christian slave in the apostle's days might have had to go down to the market on his master's business; but you may be sure that the Christian slave who knew what it was to be espoused to Christ would turn away as quickly as possible from the tumult of the market and the idle gossip of the street, and the harangue of the political orator would have little charm for his ear. Some have said, "But I can hear and read things without being damaged by them if I do not allow them to have a place in my heart". A very pertinent question for such persons would be, "What gain is there in occupying the mind with so much that is acknowledged to be unworthy of the heart?" But it is precisely in this way that the heart is drawn aside. The mind - the thoughts - are turned to things here, and the affections soon follow in the same direction. Nor is it a question of the actual retention in the memory of the things that are heard or read, but of the impression that is made on the mind, and the cast that is given to the thoughts by them. The mind is turned back to things here, and the speedy result of this is that the whole-hearted affection to which Christ was everything is lost, and perhaps soon regarded as only a temporary excitement of no practical value. Ah! the Lord looks back to those hours of holy joy, of absorbing affection, of burning love; and He says, "I remember thee, the kindness of thy youth, the love of thine espousals". Eight hundred years had passed in Israel's history - long centuries of backsliding and rebellion - but the Lord never forgot the brief moment in which He was everything to their hearts. How far has He to look back to find such a moment in your history or mine?

Then there is another thing. "My people have committed two evils; they have forsaken me, the fountain of living waters, and hewed them out cisterns, *broken cisterns, that can hold no water*" (Jeremiah 2:13). In the East a man sometimes spends years in hewing out a cistern in the rocks, hoping to get it filled in the rainy season, that he may have a supply for the time of drought. At last the rains descend, the streams rush into the mouth of the cistern, but the water-level does not rise - the water runs out as fast as it runs in - it is a broken cistern. What a disappointment! The man has two counts to the bad - he has wasted all his labour, and he is dry. That is God's picture of a man whose heart has been turned away from Christ. You are looking to find the present satisfaction of your heart in earthly things, but, depend upon it, sooner or later you will find that all your cisterns here are "broken". What a solemn thing to have to look back at the end on a wasted life! How sad to be dry with such a Fountain near!

I will now turn to one or two scriptures which bring before us the ways of the Lord in His restoring grace, when the hearts of His own have got away from Him. And in connection with this I may say that we are as dependent on the Lord for restoration when we wander, as we were at the beginning for salvation. How sweet to know that He does not, and will not, give us up. The secret of all His gracious dealings with us lies in the fact that He loves us, and nothing but love will satisfy love. He is jealous over us; He must have the affection of our hearts; He values it; it is the chosen satisfaction of His love.

In bringing about restoration the Lord makes use of two great agencies - ministry and government; or to put it in simpler words, He reaches us by His voice or by His hand. I am not forgetting His advocacy with the Father, for this lies behind it all. He takes up our whole case with the Father before there is a movement of restoring grace towards us, or any response to that movement in our souls. That advocacy, which is in all the value of His own nearness to the Father and based upon His sin-atoning work, is the unfailing outcome of His love. Our sin becomes the immediate occasion for His love to concern itself on our behalf, and this with the Father. Then, consequent upon this perfect and prevailing advocacy, there is the activity of His restoring grace toward us, and it is of this that I now speak.

"I know thy works, and thy labour, and thy patience, and how thou canst not bear them which are evil: and thou hast tried them which say they are apostles, and are not, and hast found them liars: and hast borne, and hast patience, and for my name's sake hast laboured and hast not fainted. Nevertheless I have against thee, that thou hast left thy first love. Remember therefore from whence thou art fallen; and repent, and do the first works; or else I will come unto thee, and will remove thy candlestick out of his place, except thou repent" (Revelation 2:2-5). Here we have ministry, or the Lord's voice, addressing itself to those whose hearts had left their first love, and seeking to call them to repentance. How solemn is the picture here presented to our view. We see an assembly that was apparently in the most perfect outward order, and in which was found an extraordinary measure of faithfulness and spiritual energy, yet lacking the one thing which alone would satisfy the heart of Christ. No human eye might have been able to discern that anything was lacking; there was service, fidelity, suffering for Christ's name's sake, and endurance of no ordinary kind. If we knew such an assembly we should probably think they were everything that could be desired. But the love of their espousals had waned; they had left the bright "first love" to which Christ Himself was everything. Alas! it is possible for our service, our fidelity, and our testimony for Christ to become prominent in our minds, and for these things, so excellent in themselves, to usurp the place which Christ longs to hold in our affections. It may have been so at Ephesus, for Satan will use even such things as these to corrupt our minds from simplicity as to the Christ, and it is often thus that the decline of affection begins.

How touching is that word, "Remember from whence thou art fallen". We have already seen how the Lord remembers the "first love" of His saints; He delights to call it to mind; and He counts upon it being also a sweet memory to the hearts of His own. This is the first effort of His restoring grace - to recall the memory of those precious hours when the holy rapture of "first love" filled the heart, and He was really everything to the soul. Are the best and brightest seasons of your soul's history somewhere far behind? Have you to look back through the mist of intervening years to find a moment of deep joy in which Christ filled the whole vision of your soul, and His love satisfied every longing of your heart? Sorrowfully, but in tender love, the Lord calls you now to "remember". Do not allow yourself to be deceived by the fact that you know more, and that many truths are clearer to your mind. This may be so, while the affections wither, and the soul is as dry as the desert sand. May the voice of the Lord really reach and recall in power every heart that has left its first love.

"And repent". I think there is an immensity of grace in that word. It opens the door for the aroused heart to trace its way back to the point where the decline began. It is, so to speak, the Lord inviting us to return to the happiness and intimacy of "first love". It is sad and humbling that the Lord has to use such a word to His own, but there is precious grace and comfort in it for the exercised heart. Instead of putting any difficulty or discouragement in the way of our return, He invites us - calls upon us - to retrace our steps. Yet we must needs return in a way that really sets us free in the presence of His love from the things that had diverted us from Him. Hence He says "Repent". It is by the judgment in His presence of the whole course by which our hearts have wandered that we are brought back to the point where the decline began. The soul has to travel back over its course, and to judge in the presence of the Lord the true character of the things that have turned it aside, and in doing so to judge itself for the condition which gave these things their power over it. This is a deep, solemn, searching process, but infinite love calls us into it, and will carry us through it if we respond to that call. I can quite understand a backslider saying, But my course has been so crooked and intricate that I could never trace it out; and the beginnings of my decline were so subtle, and the stages of it so imperceptible that I am quite at a loss. This may serve to prove to you that you cannot restore yourself. The Lord alone can lead us back over the history of our souls, and if our hearts really turn to Him He will do it. He can show us exactly what turned us aside, and what it was that prepared us to be turned aside, and He can give us His own judgment about it all. There is no legal effort about this, but the soul sitting down before the Lord to judge with Him the whole course of departure. The result of it is that we are brought back, with a deepened knowledge of self and a truer judgment of the world, to find our entire satisfaction in the unchanging love of His heart. We are brought back to the freshness and simplicity of that "first love" to which Christ is everything.

But there is another agency employed by the Lord to reach the consciences and hearts of His backsliding people, and that is government. To bring this before you I will read from the Old Testament. "Therefore, behold, I will hedge up thy way with thorns, and make a wall, that she shall not find her paths. And she shall follow after her lovers, but she shall not overtake them; and she shall seek them, but shall not find them: then shall she say, I will go and return to my first husband; for then was it better with me than now" (Hosea 2:6,7). Here we see the movement of the Lord's hand in restoring grace. He will not allow the backslider to go unchecked in his self-chosen way; He hedges it up with thorns, and builds a wall across it. Do not our hearts know something of this? We thought to take a seemingly pleasant path, but Christ was not before our hearts when we entered it, and every step in it was taking us further from Him, and in His grace He put a hedge of thorns across it. He allowed our path to land us in painful circumstances, and the thorns tore our fresh. Did we consider that it was restoring grace which thus hedged up our way? Then again, we thought we saw a straight, smooth way before us; it fell in with our wishes, our judgment approved it, and we entered on it with the greatest assurance. But presently we came to a dead block; there was a wall right across the road, and we could neither get over it nor round it. Ah! it was restoring grace which built that wall, and which seeks to remind us by it that Christ was not before us when we turned that way.

Have you ever pursued an object without any success, and been mortified by the disappointment? Or, having obtained the desired end, found it very different from what you had expected? Have you never sought gratification in things here, and been surprised that they yielded so little? You have followed without overtaking, and you have sought without finding. You have been proving that the cisterns here are broken and can hold no water. Does not the dealing of the Lord's hand with you constrain you to say, "I will go and return to my first husband; for then was it better with me than now"?

Let us read further. "Therefore, behold, I will allure her, and bring her into the wilderness, and speak comfortably unto her" (margin, "to her heart") (Hosea 2:14). If our affections are true to Christ, they will make this world a wilderness to us; but if our affections do not make it a wilderness, His government will. He loves us too well to allow our hearts to nestle here; and He makes us conscious that it is a wilderness that He may have opportunity in our loneliness and our sorrow to speak to our hearts. The Voice that could not be heard in the din and bustle, and amid the laughter of the city, can be heard in the silence and solitude of the wilderness. Have you never had a wilderness interview with the Lover of your soul?

Then further. "And I will give her her vineyards from thence, and the valley of Achor for a door of hope" (Hosea 2:15). How significant is this! The valley of Achor (trouble) was the place where Achan was stoned, and he and his family, and his ill-gotten spoil, were burned with fire. This is very remarkable, for the sin of Achan was the first movement of departure after the people got into the land, and the place where that first movement was so thoroughly judged is the place given as a "door of hope" for a backsliding people. Does it not again impress upon our hearts the solemn and imperative necessity of judging the *root* and secret cause of the first symptom of decline! It is the allowance of the flesh - the toleration of its tastes and tendencies - which is the root of all. We allow ourselves to be swayed by a man who thinks more of a "goodly Babylonish garment", or a little silver or gold, than he does of Christ. You may depend upon it that if Christ loses His place in our affections, we are henceforth controlled either by the lust of the flesh, the lust of the eyes, or the pride of life. May the Lord conduct each backsliding heart through the valley of Achor, and give each one a thorough root-judgment of the flesh and the world.

A few words more. "And she shall sing there, as in the days of her youth, and as in the day when she came up out of the land of Egypt ... And I will betroth thee unto me for ever... I will even betroth thee unto me in faithfulness: and thou shalt know the Lord" (Hosea 2:15; Hosea 2:19,20). What a triumph of grace! Poor backsliding Israel, after more than 3,000 years of wandering and rebellion, will be brought back to the kindness of her youth, and to the love of her espousals. She will know Jehovah in His infinite grace as she has never known Him before - no longer as her Master, but as her Husband (see verse 16) - and she will enter afresh and for ever into the joy of her betrothal to Him. Beloved brethren, if this is the manner of His grace to Israel, surely our hearts are entitled to appropriate its sweetness to ourselves, who are called, through infinite love, to know Him in a closer relationship. I know that when the heart has long been a stranger to the joy of first love, there is a great tendency to settle down and go on with things as they are, as though it were hopeless to expect to be restored. I am sure that if the Lord gives your heart a fresh consciousness that He really loves you, that despairing and depressing idea will be banished from your soul. You will awake to the blessed reality of the fact that He yearns over you in rich and boundless love, and that He is ready to lead you into communion with Himself in the judgment of the things that have turned you aside, and of yourself for giving them a place in your thoughts. Your heart will leap for joy to think that His love is really unchanged. Thus restored, "first love", with all that it means for you and for Him, will again fill your heart. You will sing as in the days of your youth. You will come back with a subdued and chastened spirit - with a humbled heart and a broken will - to the joy of that moment of espousal when Christ was everything to your heart.

> *O Lord, Thy love's unbounded -*
> *So sweet, so full, so free -*
> *My soul is all transported,*
> *Whene'er I think on Thee!*
>
> *Yet, Lord, alas! what weakness*
> *Within myself I find;*
> *No infant's changing pleasure*
> *Is like my wandering mind.*
>
> *And yet Thy love's unchanging.*
> *And doth recall my heart*
> *To joy in all its brightness,*
> *The peace its beams impart.*
>
> *Yet sure, if in Thy presence*
> *My soul still constant were,*
> *Mine eye would, more familiar,*
> *Its brighter glories bear.*
>
> *And thus, Thy deep perfections*
> *Much better should I know,*
> *And with adoring fervour*
> *In this Thy nature grow.*

Still sweet see 'tis to discover,
  If clouds have dimmed my sight,
When passed, Eternal Lover,
  Towards me, as e'er, Thou'rt bright.

O keep my soul, then, Jesus,
  Abiding still with Thee,
And if I wander, teach me
  Soon back to Thee to flee.

That all Thy gracious favour
  May to my soul be known;
and, versed in this Thy goodness,
  My hopes Thyself shall crown.
                              J. N. Darby

———

THE COMFORTER
John 14, John 15, John 16

It is a very blessed thing to know that there is a divine Person here to maintain us for Christ. In the first place to maintain us in affection for Christ; then to maintain us in testimony for Him in the scene of His rejection; and thirdly, to bring our hearts consciously into the knowledge and ineffable joy of the Father's counsels.

I am sure that if the question were put to the youngest believer here, Do you desire to be in this world for Christ? a chord would be struck in his heart. I think the youngest believer would say, Yes, by the grace of God I do desire to be here for Christ. Well, it is a great thing to have such a desire, because it shows that we love Him. We may feel that we are poor, weak things, and if we think of ourselves we are so indeed. But what a comfort to know that there is a divine Person here competent to maintain us for Christ in this world.

"If ye love me, keep my commandments. And I will pray the Father, and he shall give you another Comforter, that he may abide with you for ever". This is the first mention, I believe, in the gospel, of the disciples' love for the Son of God. And He prays the Father for the gift of the Comforter in distinct connection with the fact that there is a company here of those who love Him. Now, I say to the youngest believer here, the very fact that you desire to be here for Christ shows that you belong to the company of those who love Him. You may be the smallest one in the company, but you belong to the company. If you know Him as the One who has brought every blessing to you, and secured it for you by His death, you cannot help loving Him. I believe the first awakening of love to the Son of God is when He establishes a personal link between Himself and our hearts. I trust that most here tonight know something of it. If you want it in this gospel, I would suggest the words, "He calleth his own sheep by name" (John 10:3). He establishes a personal link between Himself and hearts in this world. That is the great thing. It is not a question of how much doctrine we know, but how much are our hearts exulting with great joy in the blessed fact that a divine Person, the Son of God, has made us conscious of His love! Think of Him coming into this world to bring to us all the favour, and blessing, and joy that divine love could offer, and securing it for us by an act that puts the seal of His love for ever on our hearts! He went into death that His love might be known by our hearts! "The good shepherd giveth his life for the sheep". It is in the apprehension of this that we become conscious of His love. Not that we can compass the blessedness of it, but we are brought into it, like tiny thimbles let down into an immeasurable ocean, and it becomes our distinction and glory - the cherished satisfaction of our hearts - that we are loved by Him. The effect of this is that we love Him; we cannot help it. When the Lord Jesus was here I have no doubt His disciples loved Him. They might not be very intelligent, as we should say. But I believe what marked them, and made them precious to the Father and to Him, was that they were conscious of His love, and they were bound to Him in affection. You may see it in Peter, when the Lord said, "Will ye also go away?" Peter answered, "Lord, to whom shall we go? Thou hast the words of eternal life". He was indispensable to them; He comprised everything for their hearts; outside Him there was positively nothing. Beloved brethren, in what measure is it so with ourselves? Has He so put the seal of His love on our hearts - so established His love there - that He has become everything to us, and all outside Him is a blank? We may see the same thing in Thomas. We speak sometimes of his unbelief, but let us not forget his devotedness. He said, "Let us also go, that we may die with him". Do you not think he was conscious of being loved? I am sure the disciples were conscious of being loved by the Person who was in their midst. He had brought divine love to them.

In John 14 the Lord regards His disciples as a company in whom there is response to His love, and He says, "If ye love me, keep my commandments. And I will pray the Father, and he shall give you another Comforter". The gift of the Comforter is in distinct connection with the fact that we love Him, and it is the blessed mission of the Comforter to maintain our hearts in affection for the absent One.

At this point I should like to say that there are three things from the influence of which we need to be delivered, in order to be here for Christ. They are brought before us in chapters 12, 13, 14. That is the world, the flesh, and the whole sphere of sight. If we are not delivered from the influence of these things they will greatly hamper us, and hinder the response of our hearts to divine love. In John 12 the world is judged, in John 13 the flesh is exposed, and in John 14 there is nothing left in the whole sphere of sight to command our hearts, because the Person who has made Himself everything to us has gone out of it. It is a very great thing for us to be in the good of this threefold deliverance - to be in heart and spirit free from the influence of the world, and the flesh, and the whole sphere of sight. It is only as thus delivered that we can be in the power and current of the Spirit here for Christ.

The world is a great system with all kinds of ramifications, and behind it is all the power of Satan, who is its god and prince. It is the whole system of things which obtains here, in which there is nothing that is of the Father or that responds to Him. It is an immense thing to know that system as a judged thing. The Lord says in John 12, "Now is the judgment of this world; now shall the prince of this world be cast out". I understand that to mean that every element of the world has been brought to light and shown up in its true colours. All the perfection of the Son of the Father has been here, and there was nothing in the world that answered to it. On the contrary, its hatred of the Son and of the Father came out in full display. The world may seem very attractive with its vast political machinery, its great educational schemes, and its philanthropic institutions; but, beloved friends, it is exposed for those who love the Son of God in the very fact that it has rejected Him. For those who love Him the world is thoroughly exposed; we have no respect for its pretensions; our hearts have broken with it and are free from its influence, because the Person who has made Himself everything to us has not found a bit of response in it.

Then the flesh is thoroughly exposed in John 13. It comes out in Judas in the most awful form, as being just material for Satan. Satan understands the flesh perfectly; he is master of all its intricacies and he can do anything he likes with it. And in Judas we see what the flesh is capable of when it is allowed to take its own course. For the sake of a paltry gain he would betray the Lord. Then in Peter we see the flesh in what might be called its best form.

In Judas we see it in its worst form, but in Peter it is the flesh taking credit to itself for its constancy and its power to suffer for Christ. And what becomes of it? It completely breaks down. Beloved friends, we have to learn that the flesh is a thing that will break down. We cannot trust it for a minute. It is sure to break down. The flesh may set up to be energetic in service, to be profound in humility, to be intelligent in the things of God, to be devoted in affection to Christ, or to be eminent in spirituality. But, sooner or later, it will break thoroughly down. I trust that none of us would care to go on with something that is sure to break down in the end.

Then in John 14 the Lord says, "Let not your heart be troubled: ye believe in God, believe also in me". That is, He was going out of the sphere of sight, but as an unseen Person He would have His own to be linked with Him in faith and love. When He was with His disciples He so commanded their hearts that they were delivered from the power and influence of other things, and now as the unseen and absent One He would carry their hearts with Him entirely outside the range of seen things. If we are influenced and controlled by things which are seen, we come under the power of things in which Christ has no place. He has gone out of the sphere of sight, and the question is, How far has He carried our hearts out of it with Him? It is a great thing for us to be in some measure delivered from these things, for it is only as we are thus delivered that we really enter into the thoughts of divine love.

The Son of God has brought divine love here. As we read in John 13:1, "Having loved his own which were in the world, he loved them unto the end". Everything that is not the outcome of divine love will break down sooner or later, and we do well to take this to heart. But there is something that cannot break down - that cannot fail - and that is divine love. I am sure the effect of knowing even a little of this love is to greatly draw us to the blessed Person who has brought it to us. A taste of it makes us long for more, and we are thus drawn to Himself.

I have no doubt that every young believer here knows what it is to pray. You pray about your pathway, about difficulties and changes in your circumstances, about your trials, and your service. But I should like to ask, Do you know what it is to get near to the Lord Jesus Christ the Son of God, that He may lead your heart into the blessedness of His own love? He may give us a taste of that love, as it were, at a distance, but it is in order to draw us to Himself, that we may learn it fully in His own company. Satan will do his best to divert us by all possible means from entering into this, but if our hearts have really come under the power of divine love we shall not be diverted. John had come under the power of that blessed love, and responded to it, leaning on

Jesus' bosom. It seems to me that John 13 is the school of love. The Master teaches divine love in perfection; the disciple learns with his head pillowed on that Master's bosom; and the result of the learning is that the disciples can be told to "Love one another as I have loved you".

What a wonderful thing it is to get into His company to learn there how He loves; because His love does not ignore what the flesh is, nor does it forget our liability to be influenced and defiled by what is around us here. Yet He loves, and loves to the end. It is a blessed thing to know that His love has secured to itself the title to regard us apart from everything that is unworthy of that love. He has gone into death to remove from us divinely and for ever all traces of unsuitability to Himself. His death has set Him free, if we might say so, to love us, and as we appropriate His death it sets us free to be loved. On His side love is free, and as we appropriate His death we appropriate that which sets us free in spirit from all the sin and imperfection of the flesh, and we are free to be loved. The Lord Jesus looks upon us according to the thoughts of His love, and according to the perfect sanctification of His death, and thus apart from every trace of imperfection. When He "loved the church and gave himself for it", do you think He saw it in guilt and ruin? No, He saw it in its beauty, according to the thoughts of His own love. For us to enter into this there must be the appropriation of His death, and this sets us free to be loved. There can be nothing more blessed than to be free to enter into the love of divine Persons. It is eternal life, and the effect of it comes out in love one to another. Thus the saints are bound together in affection. It will be so perfectly and for ever in the Father's house. All hearts there will be full of divine love, and bound together in that love by the all-pervading Spirit. What a wonderful thing that we may taste a little of it even here.

In John 14 the Lord says, as it were, While I have been with you I made you conscious of My love, and made known to you the thoughts of My love. Now I am going away, but another divine Person will come to you to maintain in your hearts the link which I have formed. He will maintain in your remembrance the communications of love by which I attach you to Myself. He shall teach you all things, and bring all things to your remembrance, whatsoever I have said unto you. No doubt this applies in a special way to the apostles, but in principle it is true for the whole Christian company. A young believer might say, If I could have been with the Lord I am sure He would have made me conscious of His love, and I should have known that love much better than I do now. Well, beloved friends, the Comforter has come to maintain in our affections those blessed communications by which the Son of God established the knowledge of His love in the hearts of His little company of disciples when He was here with them. Those communications included His "commandments" and His "word". We read in verse 21, "He that hath my commandments, and keepeth them, he it is that loveth me". And in verse 23, "If a man love me, he will keep my word". As I understand it, His "commandments" are the expression of the pleasure of His love concerning His own, and His "word" is the expression of all that He is in Himself. He says, "This is my commandment, That ye love one another". That is the pleasure of His love concerning us, and if we love Him we keep His commandments. They are attractive to our hearts; they win their way into our souls and are treasured, there; and they draw us in a very blessed way to Himself. Then his "word" expressed what He was in Himself; it established the knowledge of Himself in the hearts of the disciples; they knew Him in His own blessedness; they contemplated His glory. He says, "These things have I spoken unto you, being yet present with you. But the Comforter, which is the Holy Ghost, whom the Father will send in my name, he shall teach you all things, and bring all things to your remembrance, whatsoever I have said unto you". That is, the Comforter comes to maintain our hearts in those blessed affections which were formed by the communications of His love. Beloved friends, how far have we been in the good of the presence of the Comforter? He is here to maintain us thus in affection for Christ, and if we are set for Christ there is no doubt He will thus maintain us. May the thought of it be real encouragement and strength for our hearts!

Now a few words as to the Spirit being here to maintain us in testimony for Christ. We are left here for the testimony of Christ. When He came here, sent by the Father, He brought into this world everything that was perfectly suited to the Father. And He was hated, persecuted, and cast out, because the world did not know the One who sent Him. "Now they have both seen and hated both me and my Father". All the power of the world and Satan - all the power of evil - was put forth to get rid of Him, but, beloved friends, they did not get rid of the testimony which He brought here. And no power of evil can dislodge the testimony of God from this world. It was brought here by one divine Person, and set forth in Him in absolute perfection; it is maintained now in the saints by another divine Person - by the Comforter. People may get occupied with the ruin and failure of things until they get completely discouraged in heart. There is immense power in getting to God's side of things, and in seeing that there are things which cannot break down, because they subsist in the power of divine love and by the Spirit of God. It is certain that everything else will break down; everything that has not its outcome from divine love, and that is not in the power of the Spirit, will break down. But the Comforter will maintain the testimony of Christ here, and it is surely the chief concern of our hearts to be in the line of that testimony. The Comforter did not come to add to the testimony. When the Son of God was here the testimony was complete; nothing could be added to what He brought; He set forth all the blessed light and grace of the Father here, and everything that was perfectly suited to God and the Father in a man shone out in Him. And now another divine Person comes from the Father to maintain that same testimony in the church, the body of Christ.

The Comforter is here to maintain us in the power and grace of the wonderful testimony that came out in blessed perfection in the One sent from the Father. It came out in all its heavenly grace and beauty in Him. There may be correctness in life and doctrine, with very little display of the grace of Christ. Many believers have a line they would not care to step over; they would not like to do anything they had a conscience about; they are outwardly correct in life, and they are orthodox in doctrine. But there may be all this without much true testimony - without much expression of the grace of Christ; there may be very little in it to give real satisfaction to the Father. In the blessed Son of God everything was divinely right - it could not be otherwise - but everything was in such exquisite grace that it was infinitely acceptable to the Father, and the Father's grace was perfectly expressed in it. This is true testimony. How small the consideration of it makes us feel.

I believe if we settle down with mere outward correctness the world will approve us. The world can get on very well with a Pharisee, for he is of the world; but I am sure the world will never appreciate the grace of the Father - it will never appreciate the testimony. If we are here really in the grace of Christ, I am sure people will not understand us. They will say that we are fools and not fit for this world. The world can never understand the wonderful grace which was shown out here by the One who came from the Father, and it is the expression of that grace which constitutes true testimony now, and the Comforter is here to maintain us in it. The subjects of John 15 are fruit and testimony. Fruit is for the Father, and only that which is fruit for the Father is testimony in the world.

I come now to chapter 16, where the Comforter is promised as the One given to lead us into the knowledge and joy of the Father's counsels. "Howbeit when he, the Spirit of truth, is come, he will guide you into all truth: for he shall not speak of himself; but whatsoever he shall hear, that shall he speak: and he will show you things to come. He shall glorify me: for he shall receive of mine, and shall show it unto you. All things that the Father hath are mine:

therefore said I, that he shall take of mine, and shall show it unto you". The Son has an equal interest with the Father in the carrying out of the Father's counsels. It is the distinctive glory of the Father to originate those counsels, and it is the distinctive glory of the Son to give effect to them. And we, marvellous to say, are brought into a circle of things which could only be originated and carried out by divine Persons - a circle of things where everything is the outcome of divine love. How could we enter into such things without the Comforter! It would be impossible. "I have yet many things to say unto you, but ye cannot bear them now". But, thank God, what He could not say to the disciples He could say to the Father in the marvellous language of John 17. He could lift up His eyes to heaven and say to the Father in their presence what He could not say to them. And we are privileged to stand by and hear one divine Person speaking to another, and occupied about us who are brought in infinite love within the circle of the Father's counsels. And not only so, but the Comforter has come to lead us into the knowledge of those counsels, and into the ineffable satisfaction and joy of the divine love which has originated them, and which will give effect to them in a universe of bliss for ever.

Beloved brethren, our great distinction is that we are loved by divine Persons. One feels lost in the greatness of it. I feel that I have only begun to touch the verge of Christianity, and nothing would please me better than for every one in this room to go away impressed by the fact that there is very much in it that our hearts have not yet been conducted into. It is an immense comfort that the Holy Ghost has come, and that it is His blessed mission to guide our hearts into the knowledge of the Father's counsels. I cannot attempt to unfold those counsels, or to do more than suggest one or two thoughts in connection with John 17.

The ground on which all is effected is, "I have glorified thee on the earth. I have finished the work which thou gavest me to do". Then in verse 1 the Son asks to be glorified, that He may glorify the Father. And He brings about the Father's glory by giving eternal life to as many as the Father has given Him. It is the Father's glory to have a company of many sons capable of appreciating Himself. It is His glory to have a company of worshippers before Him. Worship is the appreciation of divine Persons, and the appreciation of divine Persons in creatures must be adoration. He would have us as sons before Him - as those who have sprung out of the death of Christ, as those who are the "much fruit" of that precious Corn of Wheat in new creation suitability to the Father's presence. It is the very glory of the Father to have such a company. And the Son has glorified Him, and is glorifying Him, by securing that company - by giving them eternal life. Then lower down in the chapter we find that the saints are also the glory of the Son. He says, "I am glorified in them". It is a marvellous thing that we should have been taken up, and enriched and blessed by divine love, so that the glory of the Father and the Son should be displayed in us. The Church is the vessel of divine glory. "To him be glory in the church". We belong to the vessel in which divine glory will be displayed for ever. And the Comforter is come to lead our hearts into these things, and to maintain the knowledge and the joy and the ecstasy of them in our hearts. If we enter into these things we must be beside ourselves.

In the circle of divine love we are outside the range of the natural man altogether; we are in a region where nothing can sustain us but the Comforter, and He is here for that purpose.

Then the consummation of everything is that we are to be with the Son where He is, to behold His glory which the Father has given Him - a glory connected with the love which the Father had for Him before the foundation of the world. We are to be introduced to a scene where we shall know what one divine Person can be to another, and how one divine Person appreciates another. We shall find the eternal joy and rapture of our hearts in knowing what the Son is to the Father, and in knowing the Father according to the blessed revelation of His Name made by the Son. "I have declared unto them thy name, and will declare it: that the love wherewith thou hast loved me may be in them, and I in them". And the Comforter is given to show us things to come - to give us now "as heavenly light what soon shall be our part".

I desire for my own heart, and for every saint of God in this company, that we should know the presence of the Comforter as a great reality. He is here to make these things real for our hearts. If we are really set for Christ, I am sure we may count upon the Comforter to maintain us in affection and in testimony for Him. And if we are responsive to divine love, He will guide us into the knowledge of those counsels in which the blessedness of that love reveals itself. May God bring the light and joy of these things a little more into our hearts!

THE CHRISTIAN'S DESIRES:
AN INDEX TO CHRISTIAN CHARACTER

I wish to bring before you tonight a most interesting subject, viz., The Desires of a Christian. A man's true character comes out when you get to know his desires. If you knew a man's desires you would know the man; they are the true index to what he is. What a man has or what he is outwardly does not constitute his character: for this you must go beneath the surface to the hidden springs of the heart. In the Word of God man in the flesh is exposed right down to the very roots of his being. Not only is divine light thrown upon his actions and words, but the very desires of his heart are dragged out from their secret hiding-places and exhibited in their true and hideous nature, so that we know not only what man has done, but what he is - we know his character.

In a similar way we have in the Epistle to the Philippians the unfolding of the desires of a Christian's heart; and in connection with this I may remark that nothing is more wonderful than the way in which God developed the life and experience of a Christian in the beloved Apostle Paul, so that the most exalted truths are not here stated in a doctrinal way, but are presented as having been worked out in the life and experience of a man subject to like passions as we are. In this epistle the heart of the man in Christ is uncovered, the very core of his moral being is laid bare, his inmost desires are exposed, and thus we learn here not so much what are the privileges, or the activities of the Christian, as we learn what constitutes the character of a Christian. May the Lord's blessing attend our meditations on this subject!

1. "According to my earnest expectation and my hope, that in nothing I shall be ashamed, but that with all boldness, as always, so now also, Christ shall be magnified in my body, whether it be by life, or by death" (Philippians 1:20).

Consider for a moment the peculiarly trying circumstances in which Paul was found when these words were penned. Think of him with all his natural energy of character, and with all the burning desires of a heart that had been saturated with the love of Christ, and longed to carry the fulness of the blessing of Christ to every saint and sinner under heaven; and think what it must have been to him to be hemmed in by the four walls of a Roman prison! Such had been his position for at least two years, and yet he expresses no desire to have his circumstances altered. His one care and desire was that Christ might be magnified in his body in any circumstance - whether by life or by death.

Did you never find yourself making your circumstances an excuse for your lack of devotedness to Christ? The poor man thinks, If I were rich I could magnify Christ a great deal; the weak one thinks, If I were strong and robust, what an amount of service I could render; the one who has not much gifts thinks, If I could speak as well as So-and-so I could honour Christ much more than I do; others say, If I were in another family, If I had a different occupation, If my circumstances were changed a little, Christ might be magnified more largely in me.

Now the simple fact is that this is all self-occupation, and these are the wretched excuses made by the flesh to justify a lack of devotedness to Christ. Look at them, and you will find that they all centre round self. It is if I this, and if I that, I would be a wonderful Christian, and of course I should have the credit of it, and, in result, I would be magnified. The soul in this state has not really done with self - that wretched old I - and if circumstances permitted many works and much Christian activity, the result would be something like Job 29. If you read that chapter you will find the occurrence about fifty times of the words "I", "me", and "my". Job had been in circumstances which favoured a great deal of benevolent activity, but you notice it all centred round himself, and you might justly entitle this chapter, "*self-magnified*".

An immense advance upon this may be found in a remarkable utterance of John the Baptist; "He must increase, but I must decrease" (John 3:30). Himself one of the last and greatest saints of a dispensation which recognized man in the flesh, John was taught of God to express what was not only true of himself personally, but true of him as the representative of man in the flesh. The very presence on earth of the Second Man out of heaven was morally the setting aside of the old order of man in the flesh. Here was One who had come from above - from heaven - and contrasting this One with himself - the man of the new order with the man of the old - John says, "*he* must increase, but I must decrease". As the glories of the Person of Christ passed before the eyes of faith, He eclipsed everything that was of the first man.

Thus in Job 29 we have self-magnified; in John 3 self-decreasing, one mere step and we find self gone.

"I am crucified with Christ: nevertheless I live; yet not I, but Christ liveth in me: and the life which I now live in the flesh, I live by the faith of the Son of God, who loved me, and gave himself for me" (Galatians 2:20). At the cross the One who knew no sin was made sin for us. It was, so to speak, as the representative of the race of Adam that He died. The deep, dark waters of death flowed over and covered Him - as once they flowed over the created earth - and the end of all flesh came before God. That was the end of man in the flesh in the sight of God, and every believer in Jesus is entitled to take account of himself as having "died with Christ".

This is the starting-point of true Christian experience. When first converted I suppose we all, with more or less earnestness, endeavoured to be what we felt we ought to be. We struggled and prayed and resolved, and were grievously disappointed to find that we could not succeed in our purpose. We found that there was something within us which would not be brought into subjection to the will of God. We discovered that we had not only been guilty of doing many bad things, but that we were bad ourselves. It was not sins that troubled us at this stage of our experience, but self. At last we despaired of making ourselves better: we reached the point that another had reached hundreds of years before us, and could only cry, "O wretched man that I am! who shall deliver me from this body of death?" We became sensible that we needed as complete a deliverance from self as we did from sins. When we reached that point God showed us the blessed One who was lifted up upon the cross - antitype of the brazen serpent - and we were prepared to accept the precious truth of the gospel, that "our old man has been crucified with him", and that "we have died with Christ". We appropriated the death of Christ and reckoned it as our own; at the same time discovering that Christ as the living, risen One was our life. Now the Holy Ghost, if ungrieved, would maintain us in the liberty of "life in Christ Jesus". As we walk in the Spirit we are kept in communion with God as to "our old man", and he never comes back before God - he has been condemned and set aside for ever in the stupendous judicial act of Calvary.

Then not only does Christ live in us, but He becomes the motive Object of our life as Christians. The law is no longer our motive or rule of life. It is entirely displaced by a Person, and that Person "the Son of God, who loved me, and gave himself for me". Henceforth the soul has got a new centre - it is no longer self-centred but Christ-centred. Christ is the motive Object and not self.

The Epistle to the Philippians starts on this level. If we do not know Galatians 2:20 in our souls, we are not at all prepared for Philippians. The "I's" and "me's" of Philippians (about ninety in number) are very different from the "I's" and "me's" of Job 29 or Romans 7. It is the Christian, as such, who speaks in this epistle, and the desires and experience spoken of are those of one who knows what it is to be "a man in Christ". With such a one it is no longer a question of circumstances, or of what may happen to him; but the desire that, whatever happens to him, Christ may be magnified, becomes the supreme concern of the heart. He counts that the "old man", who would have rivalled Christ, and who desired to magnify himself, has been reduced to nothingness at the cross; and now Christ is filling the whole horizon of his faith and love. He can look at the whole range of possible circumstances - covering all by the words "life or death" - and his only desire is that Christ may be magnified in his body, whether it be by life or by death. The Christian, as such, has done with self as the source of his motives altogether.

2. "Having a desire to depart, and to be with Christ, which is far better" (Philippians 1:23).

I am afraid that in our desire to give prominence to the precious truth of the Lord's coming, we sometimes give the impression that it is a very inferior kind of thing to look for departing to be with Christ. It is therefore well that we should be reminded in this epistle of highest Christian experience that Paul had "a desire to depart". The Holy Ghost knew that in the actual history of the Church millions of believers would "fall asleep", and it was important that the attitude of the Christian in view of this possibility should have a place in this epistle. Otherwise it might be supposed - as was actually the case at Thessalonica - that to "fall asleep" was to sustain some loss, and that those alive at the time of the rapture would have some advantage over those who departed before. To be "with Christ" is "far better" than to remain here. The sweetest thought in connection with the rapture is that "So shall we ever be with the Lord" (1 Thessalonians 4:17). That is the heart's own portion, and it is a very precious fact that the infinitely blessed prospect of being in the Lord's company is connected with the departure of the Christian as well as with the coming of the Lord (see Luke 23:43; 2 Corinthians 6:8; Philippians 1:23). The Christian's heart longs for the company of the Glorious One "who died for us, that, whether we wake or sleep, we should live together with him". Therefore if we think of ourselves as part of the Church, we look for the Rapture; if we think of ourselves as individuals, we "have a desire to depart, and to be with Christ". Nor is this a small thing, for where this desire really exists it bears witness that the heart is not seeking its portion here - it has done with the earth. The separating word has entered the soul - "Arise ye, and depart; for this is not your rest: because it is polluted". The mind is set on things above, not on things on earth. The links with heaven are stronger than the links with earth, and the soul's desire is there, not here.

I am afraid, beloved friends, that sometimes we look upon death as a melancholy termination of our course upon the earth. There is, I fear, but little of this leaping forward of the heart to be "with Christ". Paul does not speak of resignation or submission; he expresses a desire that burned with fervour in his soul. The earth was for him the poor polluted scene of man's sin and Satan's power, and he longed to be away from it "with Christ". The only thing that detained his heart here was the church. Christ's treasure - the members of His body - was here, and for their "furtherance and joy of faith" he was willing to remain. The Christian, as such, has no object upon this earth but the interests of Christ.

3. "That I may rejoice in the day of Christ, that I have not run in vain, neither laboured in vain" (Philippians 2:16).

This third desire of Paul's heart looks on to the day of Christ - the day of manifestation and reward – and a solemn possibility is suggested that his joy in that day might be diminished if the saints at Philippi - the results of his labour - did not turn out to be bright, real witnesses for Christ.

I take it for granted that you are fully established in the grace of God as to forgiveness and salvation. You know, through grace, that your sins are forgiven and that you are as clear of condemnation as Christ Himself. You have been saved by grace, and you now stand in grace, and you are assured that "grace begun shall end in glory". It is only when the heart is established with grace, that it is rightly prepared to be girded by the bands of Christian responsibility. Do not be afraid of the word "responsibility". We have a responsibility as servants of the Lord Christ, of which we shall presently give account at His judgment-seat; and this is a truth which I believe is urgently needed to ballast our souls in these days of self-seeking and self-pleasing. It is a solemn and a sobering thought for us, as responsible servants of Christ, that there is a day coming when all our service will be weighed in the balances of the sanctuary; when all our ways, words, and actions will be manifested, and even the secret counsels of our hearts exposed in divine light.

I will bring before you two or three scriptures which connect themselves with this desire of Paul that he might "rejoice in the day of Christ". (Read 2 John 8; 1 Corinthians 3:13 - 15; 2 Corinthians 5:10; 1 John 2:28.) The solemn and heart-searching possibility is suggested to us in these scriptures that we may "lose those things which we have wrought"; that we may "suffer loss"; that we may be "ashamed before him at his coming"; and depend upon it, my brethren, these are not vain words. I pray God that their solemn force may not be lost upon us.

It is very sweet to see how all this is made to act upon the affections of the saints for their spiritual fathers and teachers. In two of the scriptures which we have read, it is brought forward as a reason why the saints should behave themselves properly, as it is also here in Philippians 2. Thus the Holy Ghost enlists the affection of the saints for their spiritual fathers and leaders as a motive to godly life and spiritual progress. The saints were, in a certain way, the workmanship of the servant, and if they turned out badly it would be his loss as well as theirs. It is as though the servant said to his converts, or to those for whom he was caring in the things of the Lord, You would, I am sure, like me to have full wages for my work, and to be able to give an account of it not only without shame, but with joy. If you turn out well this will be the case, but if you turn out badly I shall suffer loss. A weaver knows very well that if he turns out a damaged piece he does not get full wages; and if the servants of the Lord turn out bad work they cannot expect to get full wages. If the servant's work is of first-rate quality it will be his glory, and joy, and crown of rejoicing in the day of Christ; but if his converts walk badly, and the lambs and sheep for whom he is caring do not thrive, he will certainly be a loser, and this is applied to the hearts and consciences of the saints as a reason why they should walk well.

We must remember in this connection that all *Christians* are "the servants of Jesus Christ". It is in this character that Paul is writing in this epistle (see Philippians 1:1); he takes ground which was not only common to himself and Timothy, but also to all saints. Even to slaves it was said, "Ye serve the Lord Christ". Whatever be the nature of our service, it will pass under review at the judgment-seat of Christ. May each of us think less of the opinions which men form concerning us in this day, and be more anxious to rejoice in the day of Christ that we have not run in vain, neither laboured in vain!

4. "But what things were gain to me, those I counted loss for Christ. Yea, doubtless, and I count all things but loss, for the excellency of the knowledge of Christ Jesus my Lord: for whom I have suffered the loss of all things, and do count them but dung, that I may win Christ" (Philippians 3:7, 8).

Paul had counted all the religious "gain" of which he speaks in verses 5 and 6 "loss for Christ", and still, after many years of deepening acquaintance with Christ, he counts "all things but loss for the excellency of the knowledge of Christ Jesus". The great desire of his heart is, "That I may win Christ", or, as it may be translated, "That Christ may be my gain". You understand such an expression in connection with earthly things; you know what James means when he speaks of buying and selling and getting gain. You know what it is to make things on earth your gain. In contrast to this, Paul was laying himself out that Christ might be his gain. He did not want gold, or silver, or religious reputation; he wanted Christ; and to gain Christ he gave up all the things that would have made something of Paul. You may have found out that your bad things are a loss to you, but Paul had discovered that his good things were a loss to him. It was the things which elevated him morally and religiously as a man on the earth that he counted loss. He had everything that could thus elevate him when he was unconverted and without Christ. A man may have an immense amount of moral and religious "gain" and yet be nothing more than a natural man - a man in the flesh. Christianity when taken up by the natural mind is a great elevation for man, and has become a great "gain" to many who do not know Christ at all. It is a solemn truth that all such "gain" is a great hindrance to gaining Christ. It is really building up the man who, as we have already seen, was set aside at the cross. Paul gave up everything that constituted his perfection as a religious man upon this earth - counting it all loss - that he might win Christ. In short, he gave up one man that he might gain Another; and this not only at some particular moment, but in such a way that this desire gave colour and character to his whole life. The Christian, as such, renounces the first man and everything that could be a gain to him, that he "may win Christ".

5. "And be found in him, not having mine

own righteousness, which is of the law, but that which is through the faith of Christ, the righteousness which is of God by faith" (Philippians 3:9).

Another great desire of Paul's heart was to be found in a righteousness that is wholly of God. What a glorious anticipation! He looked to be found in a righteousness to which the first man could not contribute a fraction. He rejoiced to escape from the possibility of any intrusion of his own righteousness. A man may be upright and amiable, and these natural qualities are often mistaken for the fruit of the Spirit. Some men are kind and conscientious who are not converted at all.

None of these natural qualities go into the new creation, any more than the opposite qualities which are found in others. In the new creation "all things are of God"; everything that could be connected with man in the flesh is displaced, for that man himself is entirely set aside. Our whole condition in glory will be the display of a righteousness which is ours "through the faith of Christ". Everything that is seen there will be of God - it will be the display to wondering worlds of what we have been made in Christ. And the Christian, as such, is looking with earnest desire to be thus found. He looks to be found completely apart from everything that could be attained by the first man, having only "the righteousness which is of God by faith".

6. "That I may know him, and the power of his resurrection, and the fellowship of his sufferings, being made conformable unto his death; if by any means I might attain unto the resurrection from among the dead" (Philippians 3:10, 11).

The knowledge of Christ in glory was the supreme desire of Paul's heart, and this desire could never exist without producing an intense longing to reach Him in the place where He is. Hence the heart that longs after Him where He is, instinctively turns to the path by which He reached that place in glory, and earnestly desires to reach Him in that place by the very path which He trod. The heart asks, How did He reach that glory? Was it not through resurrection? And did not sufferings and death necessarily precede resurrection? Then the heart says, Nothing would please me so well as to reach Him in resurrection glory by the very path which took Him there. It is the martyr spirit; Paul wanted to tread as a martyr the pathway of suffering and death that he might reach resurrection and glory by the same path as the Blessed One who had won his heart. When Christ in glory is really known the heart can not only accept, but earnestly desire to be found in, the path which He trod down here - the path which through suffering, death, and resurrection leads to glory.

To read these burning desires of a Christ-absorbed heart is - if one may speak for others - most humbling to us, but they are the normal desires of the Christian as such. You may say that very few are up to this level. Alas! it is but too true! We have grieved the Holy Ghost by our selfishness, our worldliness, our earthly-mindedness; Christ has not been paramount in our affections; our minds have not been set on things above; we have minded earthly things instead of practically having our citizenship in heaven; and the cross of Christ - His place on earth of rejection, suffering, and death - has not been coveted. Alas! many walk still of whom Paul could only speak with tears - "enemies of the cross of Christ" - those whose walk was of the very opposite character to suffering and death in this world. In contrast to all this, Paul could exhort the saints to "be followers together of me, and mark them which walk so as ye have us for an ensample". He was a friend of the cross of Christ; he cherished and coveted a path which led to glory through suffering and death.

7. "I follow after, if that I may apprehend that for which also I am apprehended of Christ Jesus" (Philippians 3:12).

Did you ever sit down in the presence of the Lord for half an hour to seek to apprehend the immeasurable glories for which Christ has taken you up? We have been apprehended of Christ Jesus; He has taken hold of us, and He is going to bring us into - what? The Christian, as such, desires to apprehend the full purpose of the love of which he is the subject. He longs to search the heights as well as the depths of that love. His heart rises into an infinitude of bliss and glory which cannot be expressed in human words. In another epistle Paul prays that the saints "may be able to comprehend with all saints what is the breadth, and length, and depth, and height" - but he leaves the sentence unfinished. The whole immensity of the glory into which divine love will bring its subjects rises before his heart, but cannot be expressed. Christ Himself the centre of that glory - the fountain of love that passeth knowledge - and from that centre streams of light and glory filling the whole universe of God with bliss; while "in the church by Christ Jesus" God will have the full glory of His love throughout all ages, world without end. Christ has apprehended us for that, and Paul desires to apprehend it. The Christian's desire is to apprehend the unspeakable glories for which Christ has taken him up. They cannot be expressed in human words. When the apostle had been caught up into Paradise, he could find no words capable of unfolding what he heard there. Human words cannot be freighted with the bliss and glory of that eternal future with Himself for which Christ has taken us up. May the Holy Ghost form in our hearts more intense desire to follow after and to apprehend these things.

In conclusion, I repeat what I said at the beginning - a man's desires are the index to his character. I am sure that we cannot meditate on these desires without learning something of the character of a Christian - of the one who knows what it is to be "a man in Christ". I do not ask, Are you up to it? but I do ask, Are you not delighted to know that God is working in you to produce this character and these desires? How blessed, too, to know that He who has begun a good work in us will complete it unto the day of Jesus Christ!

———————

GOD'S WORK IN US, AND HIS WAY WITH US

Philippians 1:6; Philippians 1:19-21;
Philippians 1:27-30; Philippians 2:12-16;
Philippians 3:20-21

I suppose every reader of this epistle must have noticed that there is very little of what we should call doctrine in it. It is an epistle of experience. The apostle addresses the Philippians, not on the ground of the general facts and truths of Christianity, but on the ground of God's work in them, and I think it was a great comfort to him to be able to write to them on that ground.

In writing his first Epistle to the Corinthians he could not address them on the ground of the work of God in them. He had to address them on the ground of the facts and testimony of Christianity as it had been developed among them by himself. But when they had repented and judged themselves as the effect of that epistle, he took a different line in the second Epistle and addressed them on the ground of the work of God in them.

So in this Epistle to the Philippians. The apostle's confidence as to them was, that God had begun a work in them. "Being confident of this very thing, that he which hath begun a good work in you, will perform it until the day of Jesus Christ" (1:6). The work of God in souls may be hindered, and a great deal of rubbish may accumulate over it, but it can never be undone or set aside; and God will complete His work unto the day of Jesus Christ.

The nature of God's work in us comes out in Philippians 2:13, "For it is God which worketh in you both to will and to do of his good pleasure". I am sure it is of the greatest importance to see what is involved in this. There could neither be the willing nor the doing of God's pleasure apart from Christ, for it is in Him that God finds "good pleasure". It is by God's work in us that we desire that Christ should be magnified in our bodies. Man in the flesh is a total failure, but there is another Man in whom God finds "good pleasure". God gives us the consciousness that there is a Man in whom He finds His good pleasure, and He puts our desires and our activities on the line of that Man, and thus works in us to will and to do of His good pleasure. God's good pleasure finds its eternal rest and satisfaction in Christ. It is not only that there is a Saviour for man at his worst, but man at his best has been displaced and thrown into the shade by Christ.

Saul of Tarsus was an expression of man at his best. Perhaps we can hardly understand such a man - one who never consciously violated a command of God, one who lived in all good conscience before God, and was invested with every distinction and privilege that God could give to a man according to the flesh, so that he could say, "If any other man thinketh that he hath whereof he might trust in the flesh, I more" (3:4). He excelled every other man, and yet what does he say? "But what things were gain to me, those I counted loss for Christ. Yea, doubtless, and I count all things but loss, for the excellency of the knowledge of Christ Jesus my Lord: for whom I have suffered the loss of all things, and do count them but dung, that I may win Christ" (verses 7, 8). There you see man at his very best, with every advantage and distinction God could give him; yet Paul says, I throw all that aside as worthless, because another Man has displaced and thrown into the shade everything that was my boast and glory as in the flesh.

Beloved friends, it is by the work of God in us that we come into the apprehension of Christ as the Object of His good pleasure. It is an immense thing to see the greatness of Christianity, and to discern that everything centres in Christ! In the very opening of the New Testament, what a variety of divine testimony finds its blessed centre in Him! An angel appears to Joseph to speak of Him; there is also the testimony of the Scriptures to Him; then there was the star - light from heaven: every kind of divine testimony to that blessed One. The action of the Spirit, the ministry of angels, the witness of Scripture and light from heaven were all in harmony, and all centred in the virgin's son, Immanuel, the Christ of God. If you are interested to think of the pleasure of God, it is an immense thing to find that God has secured good pleasure for Himself in a Man; that is, in Christ.

In the beginning of Matthew, Herod is a type of the man in possession of the earth. He had the throne, though he was only the puppet of a power greater than himself. Man is apparently in possession of the earth, but he is only the puppet of a power greater than himself - the power of Satan.

A fine building in England carries the inscription carved in stone, "There is nothing great on earth but man". Man after the flesh is in possession of the earth, and he hates Christ. As soon as God's Man came in, the man of the earth, represented by Herod, would have shut the door in His face if possible. Man in the flesh does not want another Man - he does not want a Man of a divine order and of divine character; he would rather be left alone to indulge his lusts. But, on the other hand, we see God's work in Joseph and in the wise men who came from the east. Joseph - type of the Jewish remnant - received the infant Jesus, and was content to suffer with Him. He went away into banishment on account of Christ being rejected. Then in the wise men coming up from the east we see a figure of the Gentiles coming up to worship the One who was of no account at all in this world. I allude to this as an illustration of how God works in the hearts of men so that they may appreciate what is according to His good pleasure. When the Christ of God came into this world there were those who could appreciate Him, who received Him and worshipped Him and suffered with Him, and that is Christianity in picture.

It is clear that in the first place the new birth is essential for this. There is no disposition in man to receive Christ apart from the new birth; the natural man does not like Christ, he would kill Him like Herod. People think that Christian England is very different from Judæa; but man is unchanged - there is not a bit of difference really between the first century and the nineteenth; there is no place for God's Man in this world, and His rejection and death has proved it. God has to work in man to produce appreciation of Christ. Hence, "Ye must be born again". There must be a divine work in man, and a work that sets aside everything of man. A man may have been an important man in this world - a prime minister, or king; but when he is born again, what is the effect? Sooner or later he is compelled to take his place before God as nothing but a lost sinner. All his greatness, his human glory, his fancied moral excellence comes to nothing; he is just a lost sinner under death and judgment. However good he may have been, however religious, however competent, when

God touches him he finds that all that he was as in the flesh is worthless, whether moral, religious, philosophic, or whatever it may have been, all is worthless, and does not yield a bit of good pleasure to God. *It is not Christ!* If I as a man in this world had the most beautiful moral character it would not be Christ; it would only be the character of a fallen creature - of a sinner. It might be gilded and decorated, but after all it would be the character of a sinner; it would give God no pleasure.

God's pleasure centres in Christ. And in connection with the grace of God we may note two things - a divine work in man which brings to nothing all the pretensions of man, and, on the other hand, the preaching of Christ. These two things are clearly seen in this epistle. When Paul refers to the gospel, he speaks of it as the preaching of Christ, "Christ is preached; and I therein do rejoice, yea, and will rejoice" (1:18). And again in verse 27, "Only let your conversation be as it becometh the gospel of Christ". The great thing in connection with the gospel is that it is the presentation of Christ; God is pleased to set forth to man by the gospel the One who is according to His good pleasure, and I am quite sure Satan has done and will do his best to obscure that gospel. There are but very few in Christendom who have really apprehended the thought that there is an anointed Man in whom God's good pleasure is found eternally, and in whom every blessing is established for men. But those in whom God has worked the willing and the doing of His good pleasure receive Christ, and rejoice in Him. In the case of Joseph and the wise men from the east, God worked in them the willing and the doing of His good pleasure. His good pleasure was in that blessed One who had come into the world, and these men's desires and actions all found their centre in Him. In proportion as God has wrought in souls they find their object and pleasure in Christ, because He is the One who ministers good pleasure to the heart of God.

And, beloved friends, it is an immense thing to view the Lord Jesus Christ in this way, for in this way God brings us into the presence of perfection. We are brought from our own imperfection to all the blessed perfection that is found in Christ. We are brought to perfection by being brought into the presence of Him in whom perfection is, and that is Christ. Christians as such are brought to perfection; that is, they are brought to Christ. I am not speaking now of how far this may be true of individual souls, or of the mass of professors, but of what Christianity is in its own proper fulness and blessing; it is to be brought to Christ. What is the meaning of the name Christian if it does not mean one brought to Christ? And if we are brought to Christ, and appreciate Christ, and our desires are centred in Christ, have we not come to perfection? Have we not found every moral excellence and beauty in Christ? God feeds His work in our souls by the perfection of Christ; God sets Him before us, and feeds our souls upon perfection: "He that eateth me, even he shall live by me". God would feed our souls and nourish us on the perfections of Christ. And, beloved saints, do you not think that if our souls fed upon the perfections of Christ, and if we knew how to digest and assimilate those perfections into our moral being, we should become a little more like Him? That is how it works. If I am down in my soul, if I am not displaying the grace of Christ, you may depend upon it there is no way of getting me into the right current except by increasing my appetite for Christ. There is no other way, and the work of God in us must be on that line. God works in us to give an appetite for and appreciation of Christ; He works in us to enable us to feed upon the blessed perfections of the One who is the Object of His good pleasure.

In Philippians 2 He is presented as having come down here, bringing all the grace of heaven and all the perfection of His own Person into this world. And how does He behave Himself? What characterized Him in that place of humiliation! Lowliness of mind, subjection, and obedience. I often think of those words, "They are not of the world, even as I am not of the world". Beloved brethren, do we ever consider in what way He was not of the world? Scripture tells us that all that is in the world is the lust of the flesh, and the lust of the eyes, and the pride of life. That is what we are naturally; we are made up of these three defiling things, none of which are of the Father, but of the world. But look at Him, and what do we see? Divine love instead of the lust of the flesh, divine light instead of the lust of the eyes, and divine lowliness instead of the pride of life. He was not of the world. There was not a single feature in common between Christ and the world. People think Christ has come here to elevate man - to add lustre and perfection to man as in the flesh. But how could God bring the character of the heavenly One into association with the character of the earthly one - man in the flesh? They could not be made to touch at any point. One man is characterized by the lust of the flesh, the lust of the eyes, and the pride of life; and the other by divine love, and divine light, and divine lowliness. How could these two things be mingled together? Impossible! As a natural man I am a creature of self-will and lust. Could God ever have any pleasure in me? Not a bit. And there was a necessity that Christ should make an end of my history in the sight of God; for if my history had not been closed up at the cross, God could never have blessed me; I must have sunk under the weight of my own damnation into the lake of fire.

Thank God for the cross! The Man of God's good pleasure took a place on the cross where He was made *sacrificially* what we are *personally*. He was made sin, and bore the judgment of sin, and went into death, so that the whole history of the man of lust and self-will was brought to its end under the eye of God upon the cross. We were under death, and that peerless, perfect One came in love to where sin had brought us, so that our history as in the flesh might be ended in His death. But this was all in view of our being linked up with His perfection, and invested with His beauty before the eye of God for ever, and that we might be set free to feed upon all that moral beauty which has shone out so perfectly in Him.

Young believers are often greatly deceived by things in this world. We read books that deceive and hinder us. The world has its heroes and its great men - men of wonderful abilities and genius - and we may read books that speak of them, and get to admire them, and think highly of them, without pausing to ask ourselves whether God has any pleasure in them. In this way we come to admire moral qualities which are exactly opposite to the character of the lowly and holy qualities of Christ. We need a more distinct breach between our hearts and the world, and men of the world. Think of the gracious and holy character of Christ! He "made himself of no reputation, and took upon him the form of a servant, and was made in the likeness of men; and being found in fashion as a man, he humbled himself, and became obedient unto death, even the death of the cross". That is the pathway of One who yielded nothing but good pleasure to the heart of God. And God causes it to pass before our hearts that we may feed upon it, and thus He works in us the willing and the doing of His good pleasure.

Having spoken thus about God's work in us, I want now to say a few words about God's way with us. God not only does a work in us, but He has a way with us. We get a reference to this in chapter 1: 19, "For I know that this shall turn to my salvation through your prayer, and the supply of the Spirit of Jesus Christ". God's way with Paul might well have seemed strange to flesh and blood. He was a special vessel of God's testimony, the great evangelist, the great teacher and apostle; but instead of being free for his work, he was at this time shut up in prison. Had anything gone wrong? Was Paul discouraged? In no wise; for he says, "I know that this shall turn to my salvation". He was put in prison, and his career of service in a public way was brought to a close; but he was not a bit discouraged. "This", he says, "shall turn to my salvation". It was God's way with him.

I think that we all get some kind of prison. God works in us first, and then His way with us comes in to help. Nothing goes wrong; you may depend upon that. God always makes His way with us contribute to His work in us; and if God's way with us brings us into straits, it only brings us into a position where our wills are restrained from working, and this is salvation.

In reference to Paul it is with bated breath one would speak of such a distinguished servant of God; but it was the action of his will that landed him in prison; but when God allowed him to be fastened up in a place where his will and activity were checked, he says, "It is all right; this shall turn to my salvation". God's way with him was preserving him from the action of his own will; and, beloved friends, we shall find that it is so in our experience. A beloved servant of the Lord, now with Him, used often to say that if Christians were wise they might discover where their wills had a tendency to work, for it was exactly at that point God would continually check and hinder them. If you find you are always checked and hindered at a certain point, you may depend upon it that it is a point where your will has a tendency to work. You would like to go in that direction, but God says, No! And why? Because He wants you to be saved. What does salvation mean? It means deliverance from all the power of evil, and I do not know anything more evil, or that I dread more, than my own will. Salvation in a practical and experimental sense is found in being set free from our own will, so that we do the will of God A saved man is one who finds pleasure in the will of God, and does His will. If there was a man in this world who always kept the sentence of death upon his own will, and always did the will of God, God could point to that man and say, That is a saved man! All the checks and discipline of the pathway turn to our salvation in this way. We need not be frightened at God's ways with us; we need not be discouraged at all. It may be we are in prison. Perhaps you don't know what my prison is, nor I yours; but in the course of God's ways with us we have to pass through circumstances which check the action of our wills, and we cannot escape their effect. God brings these things in to check our wills, and thus to bring to pass our salvation. He thus delivers us practically from the action of that which really belongs to a lost creature.

Another thing comes in in connection with this, and that is prayer. Prayer means that there is a want in the soul - a demand for something from God, and it is consistent with God's way with us that He allows the demand to arise before He gives the supply. The supply is there before the demand arises, but God does not vouchsafe the supply until the demand arises. I suppose every Christian here has known what it was to be in circumstances where there was a real demand in his soul for succour from God. It is at such a moment that we realize the true meaning and value of prayer. It is all very well to talk of God's grace being sufficient for everything, but it is another thing to realize that we cannot get on without Him. It is then that we understand what prayer is. How beautiful is the apostle's language here! "Through your prayer". Not "through my prayer", but "through your prayer".

I think it is beautiful how he regards these Philippians as being in partnership with himself. In the early part of the chapter he thanks God for their "fellowship in the gospel from the first day until now"; and when he says, "Through your prayer", it is as much as to say, I know you will pray for me, that Christ may be magnified in my body, whether by life, or by death, and this is what I desire. They were partakers of the same grace that was in Paul. He was at the front - the special target for the enemy's power, but the reserves at Philippi were supporting him with their prayers. Both he and they felt the need; there was the demand and the supply - the "supply of the Spirit of Jesus Christ". Whenever the demand becomes a reality in our hearts, we may have the "supply of the Spirit of Jesus Christ".

Now see how this works out! The Man of God's good pleasure has been rejected from the earth and set in glory at God's right hand, and God works in His saints in this world, and by His gracious way with them He brings them to feel the absolute need of divine support, so that God's good pleasure may be worked out in them. They are in the line of God's good pleasure, and they feel the need of the supply of the Spirit of Jesus Christ in order to work it out. They pray, and then the supply comes. If we are to be here for God's good pleasure, it is not by making efforts and stirring ourselves up that it will come to pass. Confessing failure and resolving to do better for the future is not sufficient. Nothing will put us in the line of God's good pleasure but "the supply of the Spirit of Jesus Christ". We must have a fresh supply for the necessity of the day, or the hour, or the minute, and how infinite is the supply available for us! Through that supply we get inward support. That is the first effect, as it was with the apostle in 2 Corinthians 12. He prayed three times that the Lord would take away the thorn. But the Lord said, "My grace is sufficient for thee: for my strength is made perfect in weakness". He says first, "My grace is sufficient for thee". By this I understand that the Lord would give Paul such a supply of His grace that Paul would be content to be reduced to nothing by the thorn; and then when Paul was so inwardly supported that he was content to be reduced to nothing, Christ's power would tabernacle over him, and accomplish infinite results through his weakness. Having this wonderful supply the apostle could say, I will "glory in my infirmities, that the power of Christ may rest upon me".

Then there is support outwardly, as we get in the end of the chapter. "And in nothing terrified by your adversaries: which is to them an evident token of perdition, but to you of salvation, and that of God" (verse 28). The thought of salvation here, and in fact all through the epistle, is that we are for the good pleasure of God. Delivered from the working of our own will and from all that is evil in the world, we are for the good pleasure of God, and the power of God's salvation keeps us in the presence of our adversaries. We thus have the power of God, not only for inward support in our own spirits, but also for outward support, so that the adversaries around are not able to crush or dismay us, or turn us aside. The salvation of God is with us, and that is a very great thing.

God works in us so that we may appreciate what is according to His good pleasure; that is, that we may appreciate Christ; and then by His way with us He practically sets aside the activity of our own wills, so that through prayer we may receive the supply of the Spirit of Jesus Christ, and in the power and grace of this be here for His good pleasure. Then there is response to God according to chapter 2, verses 12, 13, "Wherefore, my beloved, as ye have always obeyed, not as in my presence only, but now much more in my absence, work out your own salvation with fear and trembling. For it is God which worketh in you both to will and to do of his good pleasure". It is by God's work in us that we are found in harmony with His way with us, and the result is that we come out in the blessed character of Christ, and respond to God in love and lowliness and subjection and obedience. We are set in our mind and affections for the will of God. We work out our own salvation with fear and trembling. We refuse to be diverted from that which is pleasing to God. Nothing could divert Christ. Nothing could induce Him to take a single step for Himself; He was always controlled by the Father's will. We can only enter upon such a path in the spirit of fear and trembling, because we are conscious how liable we are to be diverted from it. We do not need to fear and tremble because of the difficulties and opposition around us, but because we are sensible of our own weakness. We fear and tremble because of what we are, and so long as we do so the mighty power of God's salvation will be with us. In the path of God's will we realize that all that is of ourselves is a snare and a hindrance, and that obliges us to go on in fear and trembling and in constant dependence upon God. Because if we get out of the place of dependence we lose the secret of power, and fail to work out our own salvation.

Salvation will not be complete until we get our glorified bodies, and so we read that "our citizenship is in heaven; from whence also we look for the Saviour, the Lord Jesus Christ: who shall change our vile body, that it may be fashioned like unto his glorious body, according to the working whereby he is able even to subdue all things unto himself". That is the triumphant finish of the work of God in us; He will give us glorious bodies like the body of Christ. It is a great principle with God never to set up again a thing that sin has touched. That which sin has touched is defiled for God, and it must go. Sin has touched our bodies and made them "vile", but when the Lord comes these bodies of humiliation will be changed in a moment, and we shall have instead a house out of heaven - a spiritual body, a body that never has been and never can be touched by sin - a body like unto the glorious body of the One who is at God's right hand. The power by which Christ will subdue all things unto Himself will bring it about. Christians have already come under that subduing power morally as to their minds and spirits, and when Christ comes the vile body, the body that has been touched and dominated by sin, will be replaced by a body of glory - a body suited to new creation scenes and heavenly associations and relationships.

May God enable us to see more clearly the nature of His work in us, and of His way with us, so that we may be more spiritually diligent in working out our own salvation, while we wait for complete salvation out of the scenes and circumstances and condition where sin has been!

THE HONOUR OF TRUE SERVICE

"He that waiteth on his master shall be honoured".
Proverbs 27:18

"If any man serve me, him will my Father honour".
John 12:26

It is important for us to recognize that there may be much work without any true service. A servant is one who carries out the will and pleasure of his master. One might work hard from morning to night, but if he were not doing his master's pleasure he would be a very imperfect servant.

The first requisite in a servant is subjection; the second intelligence; the third capability. Then for all Christian service *love* is essential as the spring and motive.

We cannot be acceptable servants unless we know our master's pleasure, and for this we must wait on Him. "He that waiteth on his master shall be honoured". For an illustration of this read 2 Samuel 23:14-17.

While the royal city was possessed by the Philistines, and God's anointed was in "the hold", these three men were with him. This is the first thing. The Lord says, "If any man serve me, let him follow me; and where I am, there shall also my servant be" (John 12:26). Are we prepared to follow Him in that pathway which has taken Him outside everything here as the rejected One, and placed death between Him and "life in this world"? How can we be qualified to serve Him unless we are near enough to Him to know His pleasure? "He ordained twelve, that they should be with him, and that he might send them forth to preach" (Mark 3:14). It is sweeter to His heart, and infinitely more blessed to us, that we should be "with him", than any service that we could possibly render. To be "with him" our hearts must follow Him outside the scene of His rejection - outside the sphere of man's influence and activity. We often speak of the rejection of Christ, but are we prepared to follow Him! We read of some, that "they forsook all, and followed him". This is the spirit of the true servant. It is a blessed thing when the Spirit of God so attracts and absorbs the heart by presenting the beauty and blessedness of Christ to it, that every other object is put into the shade and loses its power. This is altogether different from the way in which monks and nuns give up the world. They think that they can shut out the world by walls and doors, but nothing excludes the world from our hearts but Christ. True sanctification is when God gives us such a knowledge of the preciousness of Christ that He becomes "the Object bright and fair, to fill and satisfy the heart". Then we are drawn to Him, to wait on His pleasure, and to learn His mind. "He that waiteth on his master shall be honoured".

It was as the prophets and teachers at Antioch "ministered to the Lord, and fasted" that they were divinely instructed as to service (Acts 13:1, 2). They waited on their Master, and were honoured. One could not truly minister to the Lord except as being in separation from that which is displeasing to Him. Hence it is written, "If a man therefore purge himself from these [vessels to dishonour], he shall be a vessel unto honour, sanctified, and meet for the master's use, and prepared unto every good work" (2 Timothy 2:21).

When we are clean, and meet for the Master's use, we can be content to wait His pleasure. He may not use us exactly as we expect, or in the particular service that we should choose, but "he that waiteth on his master shall be honoured". If we wait upon Him, He will give us distinction in the truest sense. He will make us pleasurable to Himself, and this is the highest honour.

David's mighty men were near enough to him to know what he longed for, and devoted enough to go in jeopardy of their lives to yield him pleasure. Their service was undertaken purely for David's pleasure. In itself the service was insignificant. No one was likely to appreciate it, or to see any value in it, but David. They went from him, and braved every difficulty and danger, and death itself, that they might give him pleasure, and having accomplished their service of devoted love they came back to him with the fruit of their service.

The joy of the servant is not found in publishing abroad to men what has been done, but in the consciousness that the fruit of his service is well-pleasing to the Lord. "As the cold of snow in the time of harvest, so is a faithful messenger to them that send him; for he refresheth the soul of his masters" (Proverbs 25:13). I am sure I can appeal to every heart that has tasted the love of Christ. Is it not your chief joy to refresh the soul of your Master? You love to minister according to your ability to thirsty saints and sinners. It is a joy to you to be the bearer in this dark world of "good news from a far country", which are "as cold waters" to thirsty souls (Proverbs 25:25). And in watering others you find that you get watered yourself (Proverbs 11:25). But your chief joy is to be acceptable to the Lord Jesus - to minister to His pleasure.

Mark 14:3-9 gives us an example of this in the New Testament that corresponds in many ways with the service of David's mighty men. In each case devotedness of heart prompted the service, in each case it was the outcome of nearness to the one served, and in each case it was such as to possess no value in the estimation of any save the one served. No practical end, as men would judge, was achieved in either case. God thus teaches us that a supreme act of devoted service which affords the deepest gratification to the Lord Jesus, might appear absolutely worthless if judged by a human standard. The water brought by David's mighty men was poured out "unto the Lord". No doubt many thought it wasted. But it spoke to Jehovah of devotedness to His anointed, and it secured for the three mighty men a place and a name in David's kingdom. They waited on their master and were honoured.

Mary's service was the outcome of her nearness to the Lord. She had "sat at Jesus' feet, and heard his word" (Luke 10). She had waited on her Master! Her service did not spring from a groundless impulse. It was what she instinctively felt was suited to the moment. The effect of His communications was that she became conscious that He was going out of this world, and her heart followed Him in devotedness and adoration. She would lavish her all upon Him, though none but He would understand or appreciate the service. He would understand - He would be gratified - and that was everything.

What honour was put upon her! "Verily I say unto you, Wheresoever this gospel shall be preached throughout the whole world, this also that she hath done shall be spoken of for a memorial of her" (Mark 14:9). Be assured of this, that if we wait on His pleasure we shall not lose anything. On the contrary, we shall be greatly honoured. The greatest service is not that which makes the greatest show in results here, but that which is most entirely pleasing to the Lord. We are often tested as to whether we are content to be insignificant here. Do we find our joy in being exclusively for the pleasure of Christ? That is the greatest service, and the privilege of rendering it lies open for every one of us - the youngest and feeblest as well as the mature and the gifted.

In saying these few words my desire is to encourage every young believer here - and I thank God there are so many - to seek the honour that comes from God. May each one of us wait more upon the Lord, that we may learn how to become the servants of His pleasure! Remember that word, "If any man serve me, him will my Father honour".

———

A GREATER THAN SOLOMON
2 Chronicles 9

I purpose to make a few remarks on the seven things which the Queen of Sheba saw during her visit to Solomon. I need hardly say that I do not intend to dwell on these things in a merely historical way, but as figurative of certain things which are now made good in Christianity in connection with Christ risen and glorified.

The first thing that she saw was "the wisdom of Solomon". One of the first great lessons that we have to learn in Christianity is that Christ is the Wisdom of God. This comes out in 1 Corinthians 1. We have to see that every human resource and activity has been brought to nothing. Corinth was second only to Athens as a centre of learning, and as the headquarters of different schools of philosophy; and the saints were evidently affected by the atmosphere around them, as we all are more or less. Hence the apostle found it necessary to insist that the cross set man in the flesh completely aside with all his wisdom and power. There is nothing in the cross in which man can boast. No man could boast in the fact that he was under death. Human wisdom is of no account whatever in the things of God. Yet it is deeply rooted in people's minds that a preacher must be a learned man; his mind must be trained, and so on. The cross is very little understood.

In Proverbs 8 we learn that God operated in wisdom in connection with creation and in carrying out His purpose. In John 1 we read that the Word became flesh and dwelt amongst men, and it was in Him God's wisdom was seen. Then at the cross we see man in the flesh condemned and removed in judgment, while at the same time all the blessedness of God's love is brought to light. Finally, Christ is raised and glorified at God's right hand, and HE is "the power of God, and the wisdom of God".

It follows from this that the wisdom of God does not come within the cognizance of man's natural powers. It is "hidden wisdom", "the wisdom of God in a mystery". It can only be known by the Spirit (see 1 Corinthians 2). The thought of "wisdom" is the revelation of God in all the blessedness and perfection of counsels and resources that no power of evil can baffle. The fulness of the Godhead dwells bodily in Christ the glorified Man (see Colossians 2). The effect of apprehending Christ as the Wisdom of God is to make us not only independent of man's wisdom, but infinitely superior to it. And we not only have Christ objectively as the Wisdom of God, but "we have the mind of Christ". We have a new and divine intelligent faculty by which we can apprehend the wisdom of God.

The second thing mentioned as being seen by the Queen of Sheba was "the house that he had built". Christ is the builder of everything that is for God's pleasure and glory on earth. The Father prepared the material and brought it to Him (see Matthew 16:17; John 6:37, 45, etc., etc.), and He put it together in resurrection power as His assembly (see Matthew 16:18; John 20). There is divine material and a divine builder, and the result is a divine structure.

Christ's assembly is God's house. The connection between the two thoughts is seen in Hebrews 2:11, 12. The assembly is Christ's, but He sings God's praises in the midst thereof, and this gives it the character of God's house. In Hebrews 3 Christ as a divine Person - the Son - builds the house, and is over it as Son. When we come to the house of God we find what is characteristic of Christianity, viz., that the carrying out of God's pleasure is no longer entrusted to servants - however faithful such might be, as for example, Moses - but everything is brought about by the Son. That is, everything is accomplished by God Himself in the Person of the Son. It is this which gives the character of perfection to everything in Christianity.

1 Peter 1, 1 Peter 2 gives us what may be called our side of the truth of God's house; that is, we see the different elements of the divine work by which we are constituted living stones in chapter 1, and in chapter 2 we see the effect of

that work in saints coming to the living stone so as to be built up a spiritual house. In result, God's pleasure and God's testimony are found here in the assembly.

Approach to God in the sanctuary (Hebrews 10) is the highest privilege of those who form the house of God. They are also introduced to a circle where divine satisfaction can be found, and where God's light and perfection is revealed (see Psalm 27:4). This is a subject which attracts one's heart, but which I cannot enlarge upon now. It will come before us to some extent in the next section of our subject.

The third thing which the Queen saw with admiration was "the meat of his table". I have just mentioned that in the house of God we come to a circle where divine satisfaction can be found. There is food there. In the world, the greater your desires are and the more refined your tastes the less likely you are to get satisfaction. But in the house of God, the more your spiritual desires and capacities are enlarged the more perfect is your satisfaction, for there is an overflowing provision. It is not only that grace and strength are vouchsafed to us in times of need and pressure - I trust we all know something of this - but there is that which satisfies every spiritual craving and desire of those born of God.

At every stage of our spiritual history the Spirit creates in our souls exercises and desires appropriate to our state, and by which we are prepared to appreciate that which may be known of God and of His beloved Son. Spiritual tastes and appetites are thus brought into being, which can only be satisfied by the knowledge of God. But in the food of God's house there is that which perfectly satisfies these spiritual tastes.

I apprehend that "milk" is a figure of divine grace, adapting itself to our need and weakness. It is the suited food for babes; that is, those in spiritual immaturity. But "meat" represents all that which has to do with divine purpose and counsel. It is that in which the blessedness of God Himself is set forth. This is the food of those who are full-grown, those who have come to the apprehension that flesh is worthless, and that everything for God is established in Christ risen and glorified.

Next, the Queen noticed "the deportment of his servants". The word translated in A.V. "sitting", and in J.N.D. "deportment" is generally translated "dwelling" or "habitation". I judge that the thought conveyed is not exactly how they conducted themselves, but rather the excellence of their position and privilege as being called to serve in Solomon's house. It was a most blessed position to occupy. "Happy are thy men, and happy are these thy servants, which stand continually before thee, and hear thy wisdom". They had their dwelling in the circle of Solomon's greatness and glory, and they were privileged continually to hear his wisdom. We may see in this a figure of the character of Christian blessing.

Our true blessing and joy does not consist in receiving certain things from Christ, but in being drawn to Him so as to find everything that is blessed and satisfying for our hearts in Him. Christ does not give blessings away to be enjoyed apart from Himself: He gives every blessing in Himself. The great longing of the Psalmist was expressed in the words, "One thing have I desired of the Lord, that will I seek after; that I may dwell in the house of the Lord all the days of my life, to behold the beauty [graciousness] of the Lord, and to inquire in his temple" (Psalm 27:4). And again it is written, "Blessed are they that dwell in thy house: they will be still praising thee" (Psalm 84:4).

We find the same spirit in the two disciples who heard John speak and followed Jesus. When He said unto them, "What seek ye? They said unto him, Rabbi (which is to say, being interpreted, Master), where dwellest thou? He saith unto them, Come and see. They came and saw where he dwelt, and abode with him" (John 1:38, 39).

How blessed to be drawn thus into the presence of One in whom all divine wisdom and love is revealed! The true Solomon in all His glory - "as of an only begotten with a father, full of grace and truth" - the Revealer of the Father!

How blessed to be amongst the "men" given to Him by the Father, that they may find in Him the revelation of the Father, and thus be brought into life eternal! Solomon's servants dwelt in the light of his wisdom and glory, and were happy. But what was their portion and privilege compared with ours? We may see in them, indeed, a lovely and striking picture; but it is only a picture. It is given to us, through infinite grace and love, to enter into the divine reality in the power of the Holy Ghost. May God encourage our hearts to do so!

Another thing which impressed the Queen was "the order of service of his attendants [or ministers], and their apparel". All the appointments of the house, with its different offices, and the orderly and harmonious working of the whole, revealed the wisdom and perfect administration of Solomon. In this we see a figure of the order that properly belongs to the house of God. Christendom in general has entirely departed from the divine order, having lost the sense of what that order is. The administration of the Lord Jesus, and the presence of the Spirit here, are quite unknown in any practical way in Christendom generally. Hence we find ecclesiastical systems set up, and religious officials appointed to maintain human order. On the other hand, not a few have left the organized religious bodies, and taken independent and professedly non-sectarian ground, that they might be at liberty to serve and minister in their own way. But clerical order and radical independency are alike unknown in the house of God. Everything there is under the administration of one Lord, and is in the power of the one Spirit.

The clerical system stands hopelessly condemned in the presence of 1 Corinthians 12. However great and gifted a man may be, he is only one member of the body, and he cannot possibly discharge the functions of the other members. The attempt to do so can only be a human effort, unprofitable to men and displeasing to the Lord.

The radical principle of everyone doing as he feels "led" is, if possible, a greater evil still, for it gives room for all the evils of "one-man-ministry" to be multiplied, and often subjects saints to the infliction of ministry (?) from men whose only qualifications are self-confidence, and a desire to hear their own voices.

Edification is the great end of all ministry. The saints are to be built up in the knowledge of God, Christ is to be ministered to our hearts, and the things of the Spirit presented to us. And this, not merely in a general way - the barren statement of things admitted to be true - but so as to lead us on in a deepened knowledge of God. As our spiritual capacities are enlarged we should find in the house of God a ministry that would continually help and edify us. A ministry that does this approves itself to every spiritual mind as being of God. It carries the stamp of divine wisdom and grace, and it is necessarily in the power of the Holy Ghost.

The subduing knowledge of divine Persons, and a deep sense of the greatness of divine thoughts, characterizes every true "minister". We realize that he is not seeking to make himself prominent, or to display his ability in the way he presents things. He is conscious of the greatness and blessedness of that which he seeks to present, and it is his one desire that it should become great and blessed to our hearts. We see that he is absorbed by it, that it elevates him above self-consideration, and this gives moral weight to his ministry.

The service that is of God makes divine Persons and divine thoughts prominent. In this way the knowledge of God characterizes His house, and true edification is found there. The "order of service of his ministers" is invariably on the line of edification (see 1 Corinthians 14).

One word as to "their apparel". Everything about Solomon's ministers was suitable and appropriate to their service. Their personal appearance was consistent with their high service. How important is this! People will pay little heed to the ministry of those whose personal appearance and ways are not in harmony therewith. I have heard of one who was continually speaking of being "dead with Christ", and going on with much worldliness at the same time. Such ministry only dishonours the Lord, and is a stumbling-block to souls. The apparel does not match the service!

Now we come to "his cup-bearers and their apparel". These were servants who ministered in a special way to the pleasure of Solomon. There is a higher and sweeter service than that of ministry to the saints, however blessed that may be in its place. To be able to minister to the joy of Christ is a wondrous privilege, and divine love has placed even this within our reach. It is not, indeed, that we do so by bringing what is of ourselves to Him. But as we present ourselves before Him, and as our souls enter into His deep perfections and into that blessed revelation of the Father which He brings to our hearts, and as we taste and respond to His precious and perfect love, we minister joy to His heart. We bring back to Him that which is His own, but we bring it back to Him as that which has become the life and glory of our hearts. May God by His Spirit lead us more into this peculiar and blessed ministry when we are found together in assembly!

It will be noted that there are thus three classes of servants contemplated, representing saints in three aspects. "The dwelling of his servants" sets forth the position and privilege of all saints as being in the blessing and favour of God's house. "The order of service of his ministers" speaks of all that is connected with ministry and service in the house of God. "His cup-bearers" represent saints as those whose sweet and holy privilege it is to minister to the joy and satisfaction of Christ. We get the same three classes in a familiar New Testament picture (see John 12:1-8). Lazarus sat at the table with Him, and Martha served, but Mary had the deeper and sweeter joy of so entering into His mind and responding to His love that she ministered to His joy. I do not set one class against the others, for all may be true of us in their season, but let us not stop short of the last.

Finally, the Queen of Sheba saw "his ascent by which he went up to the house of the Lord". I apprehend we have in this a figure of approach to God in the sanctuary. No doubt the approach in that day was worthy of the revelation of Jehovah's Name which had been made, and it was worthy of the one who approached. But when we come to Christianity all is so infinitely great and glorious that it transcends all types and figures. The Son has glorified the Father by placing the perfect revelation of the Father's Name before the hearts of His own. He has brought all the blessedness of God to light in the activity of His holy love. He has also, by receiving those whom the Father has drawn to Him, and by accomplishing redemption and giving the Spirit, secured a company of "many sons" to be in the light of that blessed revelation, and to respond to it. But, now that the revelation is made, and the company secured, He takes a new and wondrous place as "the firstborn among many brethren". He takes a place thus on our side, that the privilege of approach may be equal to the perfection of the revelation. He first brings out the revelation of the Father, and then He leads the sanctified company to approach as His "brethren". The revelation comes out according to the greatness of the Son, who alone could bring it; and then He takes a place, as I have said, on our side to give a perfect response to that revelation - such a response as none but the Son could give.

For us the most absolute sanctification is needed in order to approach. All that we are, as in the flesh, must go. Thank God, it has gone in the death of Christ. We can find no way of entire deliverance from the flesh save by Christ's death. I do not mean now for walk but for approach. It is "through the veil, that is to say, his flesh", that we enter into the holiest. Within the veil we are "all of one" with Christ, we are of Him - His brethren. No imperfection comes there. All is new creation, and glorious in divine beauty. There the Son sings praise, and the music of His singing fills the hearts of His brethren. Thus as of Him and with Him they approach God, even the Father. The ascent by which Solomon "went up to the house of Jehovah" was no doubt glorious, but what was it compared with the approach to God which is found in Christianity? How far excelling in moral glory is that which we are called to know! If the Gentile Queen was subdued and entranced by what she saw, so that "there was no more spirit in her", how are we affected by the realities of which she only saw dim and imperfect pictures? Is it not fitting that, with subdued spirits and enraptured hearts, we should ascribe blessing and praise to the Father and the Son?

———————

www.ingramcontent.com/pod-product-compliance
Lightning Source LLC
LaVergne TN
LVHW051629080426
835511LV00016B/2262